Computer-
Integrated
Building
Design

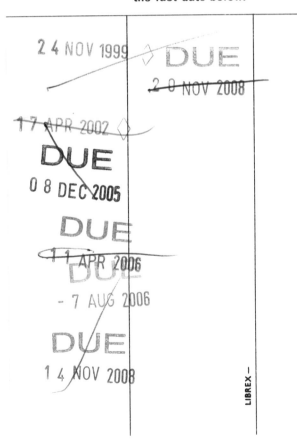

Tim Cornick

Computer-Integrated Building Design

E & FN SPON
An Imprint of Chapman & Hall

London · Glasgow · Weinheim · New York · Tokyo · Melbourne · Madras

**Published by E & FN Spon, an imprint of Chapman &
Hall, 2–6 Boundary Row, London SE1 8HN, UK**

Chapman & Hall, 2–6 Boundary Row, London SE1 8HN, UK

Blackie Academic & Professional, Wester Cleddens Road,
Bishopbriggs, Glasgow G64 2NZ, UK

Chapman & Hall GmbH, Pappelallee 3, 69469 Weinheim,
Germany

Chapman & Hall USA, 115 Fifth Avenue, New York,
NY 10003, USA

Chapman & Hall Japan, ITP-Japan, Kyowa Building, 3F, 2-2-1
Hirakawacho, Chiyoda-ku, Tokyo 102, Japan

Chapman & Hall Australia, 102 Dodds Street, South
Melbourne, Victoria 3205, Australia

Chapman & Hall India, R. Seshadri, 32 Second Main Road,
CIT East, Madras 600 035, India

First edition 1996

© 1996 Tim Cornick

Typeset in $10\frac{1}{2}$ Meridien by Photoprint, Torquay, S. Devon
Printed in Great Britain at the Alden Press, Oxford.

ISBN 0 419 19590 4

A catalogue record for this book is available from the British
Library

Library of Congress Catalog Card Number: 95–78837

∞ Printed on permanent acid-free text paper, manufactured
in accordance with ANSI/NISO Z39.48-1992 and ANSI/NISO
Z39.48-1984 (Permanence of Paper).

Contents

Preface

In writing this book, I had two main purposes. First, to demonstrate to architects, other construction professionals and clients the 'near-future' potential of reasonably low-cost computing for integrating the building-design process in their projects. In practice the aim will be to allow the design activity of each person involved in a project to be carried out simultaneously. Thus, the impact of different architectural, engineering and construction design decisions upon each other can be understood immediately and evaluated as part of the normal process. It is only in this way that each member of a project team can be assured that all the client's requirements are being met simultaneously. The computer-based tools and techniques described and illustrated in this book will bring about the realization of this aim in the not so distant future.

My second purpose is to propose that, in order for the computer to be used effectively for integrated design, an integrated project-management process must also be put in place. This may mean changes in attitude in building practice so that everyone involved is a designer; it may require procurement methods and contracts to support 'partnership' designing; the general intention will be to create building information models based upon the input of each person's special knowledge. Unless the project-management process supports the effective use of Information Technology (IT) and the methods of IT support the project management process, the benefits will not be realized. If the changes in both attitude and practice are not forthcoming, then the application of IT might have the effect of further dis-integrating a still fundamentally divided building design and construction management process.

For the purposes of logical explanation, I have used particular terms regarding the roles of those involved in a building project. The traditional roles of client, architect, engineer and specialist trade contractor are significant in terms of the generation and exchange of information, in that they still commission, design and build buildings. Absorbing the traditional roles of quantity surveyor and general contractor into that of construction man-ager is helpful when describing the input and output of informa-tion within an integrated design process, in fact the traditional procurement method in which they appear, should logically no longer exist.

Acknowledgements

I would like to thank all family, friends and colleagues whose ideas and experiences during my years of research have helped to contribute to the thinking that has gone into this book.

I would especially like to thank Bruce and Russ Noble for producing the CAD modelling for the simulated project in Chapter 8 and the Loddon School at Basingstoke for providing the 'live project' on which it is based.

Finally I would like dedicate this book to the memory of Ted Cogswell, fellow architect and former partner, who first awakened my interest in what computers would ultimately be able to do for architectural practice.

Tim Cornick
March 1995

Illustration acknowledgements

The author and publishers would like to thank the following organizations for permission to reproduce material. We have made every effort to contact and acknowledge copyright holders, but if any errors have been made we would be happy to correct them at a later printing.

Autodesk Ltd.: 5.5, 6.1, 6.2, 6.3, 6.4, 6.5, 6.6, 6.7, 6.8, 6.9, 7.1, 7.2, 7.3, 7.4, 7.5, 7.6, 7.7, 7.8, 7.9, 7.10, 7.11
Atlas: 7.10 (using AutoCAD to Speedicon)
CIM STEEL: 6.7 (using QSE), 7.4 (using QSE), 7.8 (using QSE)
Engineering Technology: 7.3 (using Reflex), 7.11 (using Reflex)
Gotch Saunders & Surridge: 7.1 (using AutoCAD)
Hans Haenlein Architects: 6.8 (using Architrion and Excell), 6.9 (using Architrion and Excell), 6.10, 6.11
HVAComp: 6.6, 7.9 (using AutoCAD)
Intergraph (UK) Ltd.: 6.1, 6.2, 6.3, 6.4, 6.5, 7.5
NHS Estates: 7.2 (using AutoCAD and MICAD)
Rover Group: 5.3 (using Computervision), 5.4, 5.5 (using Computervision to AutoCAD)
Trimco: 7.6 (using TIEMAN), 7.7 (using WINTR)

The *Simulated integrated project* (pp. 115–139) includes a series of illustrations produced using AutoCAD R12 with software packages from the following software companies:

Adobe Systems: pp. 115, 134, 135
Autodesk Ltd.: pp. 121, 122, 123, 124, 125, 126, 127, 128, 129, 130, 131, 132, 133, 134, 135, 136, 137
Asymetrix Corp.: pp. 121, 122, 123, 124, 125, 126, 127, 128, 129, 130, 131, 132, 133, 136, 137, 139
Claris: pp. 115, 117, 118, 119, 120, 134, 135, 138
Corel Corp.: pp. 115, 134, 135
Harvard Graphics: p. 139

Introduction and research background

Research objectives for computer applications

The vision of many working in the field of computer applications in architecture and construction has been for the automation of information in the architectural design decision-making process. This was based on the view that the architectural design process was by and large a question of processing information due to the large amount of data required to create a modern building. It was thought that an improvement in decision-making would come through the computer's ability to handle data and to relate the large amounts of data required to design and construct the building 'product'. In the UK, early computer applications were used in 'system' building, with its pre-defined standard components and assemblies. It was thus envisaged that construction information could automatically be generated from the design information describing a building's form and detail. This meant that when an architect produced computerized working drawings, the necessary schedules of manpower, material and plant needed for construction were produced automatically. In other words, the 2D graphical information directly generated the basic non-graphical information regarding the required construction resources.

With the demise of system building in the 1970s the interest of architectural practices in computer applications waned. Nevertheless, research into such applications continued in the academic world. The application of computers would necessitate a greater degree of discipline in the working methods of architects and those in the construction disciplines, therefore parallel areas of research that would support computer applications were also being carried out (for example, in the area of design methodologies). With the advent of artificial intelligence and expert-system computer techniques which allowed modelling and knowledge-based reasoning in the 1980s, many researchers believed that these earlier visions of the application of computers in construction would be realized. However, within architectural practices, the main interest was in the development of the potential of CAD graphics systems which were being produced by various computer systems vendors who were responding to the basic drawing and visualization needs of architects.

Under the very broad title of computer-integrated construction, two main themes of research have been developing in the academic and industrial world of architecture and construction. These are now beginning to converge, due not only to the fact that most academic research is now carried out in conjunction with industry but also that the CAD software vendors see integration as a major selling point for their future products. These two main themes of computer-integrated research are concerned with:

☐ the modelling of the products and processes of building so that information exchange between graphical and alpha-numeric systems that represent diverse knowledge domains can be economic and effective; and

☐ the technology of the CAD and related software systems, so that information processing in and between systems can become immediate and simultaneously presented with both graphical and non-graphical representations.

Over and above these main themes is the development of data exchange standards which will ensure the interoperability between one CAD vendor's system and another, particularly applicable to the transfer of graphic representations without loss of meaning. It is envisaged by both researchers and software vendors that the successful implementation of this work will ensure the production of integrated models of buildings – and not just drawings for visualization – using Information Technology.

This research focused on the way in which computer technology will in the future, through the structure of software

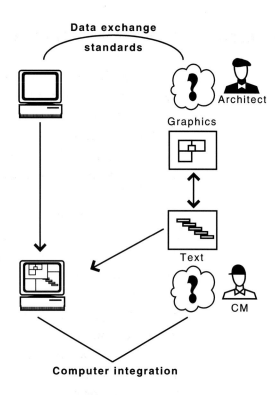

Fig. 1.1 CAD technology and building modelling research.

programmes and the configuration of hardware, allow for the integration and exchange of diverse sorts of graphical and non-graphical information generated and applied in the design and construction management of a modern building project. Examples of major European and American applied-research projects in these areas of integration and exchange are described in Appendix B.

Simultaneously, academic/industrial research has focused on the procurement methods and resources management of building projects and the structure of the construction industry itself. It has been envisaged that the actual application of IT will have a significant impact on the way in which building projects will be managed in the future. Its very application may also dramatically affect the future structure of the industry and the working practices of its traditional disciplines.

Process research and information technology

It has long been thought by both government and major private clients that the way in which the UK construction industry is structured, and the way in which projects are procured by clients, inhibits an improvement in its performance. Government-sponsored reports on the industry from the 1960s to the mid-1990s have all seemed to suggest, in one way or another, that the construction industry should become more integrated in the process of producing buildings. It is perceived that the root cause of the problems that the industry and its clients experience lie in the division of its responsibilities between the design and construction of a building. In turn these divided responsibilities are a result of the way in which the clients themselves procure their building projects and the agreements and contracts used between them and the various participants involved.

These methods of procurement and their supporting contracts and agreements are those evolved by the industry itself over the last century or so. The agreements and contracts (based on the UK JCT forms), have effectively set the various project participants in certain relationships both between themselves and their clients. In the UK, in the most common traditional method of procurement's contracts and agreements, the form and content of a legal contract has tended to encourage an adversarial approach during a building project. This created stereotypical views and attitudes by architects, engineers, contractors and sub-contractors of each other – all of which had to be overcome if the common objectives of a client's project were to be identified and realized.

The other main area of research into integration has therefore concerned the methods of procurement and the actual process of a project. The aim has been to identify, both through academic study and experiments in practice, how different project management process approaches could improve the time, cost and quality of building projects. One major new initiative introduced into the construction industry in the UK over the last decade has been the application of quality assurance as a means of trying to improve the quality of a finished building. It was hoped by both the UK government and others that the application of quality management principles taken from other industries (from QA to BS 5750/ISO 9000 and Total Quality Management) would bring about all the necessary improvements. This rather imposed demand has also generated much industry-related academic research not only into QA but also into the fundamental process of a building project itself.

This research has generated certain changes to the methods of procurement that should support an integrated management process for building projects. The procurement and management aspects of these new methods are dealt with in Chapter 3. As far as IT is concerned, the emerging computer-based systems are seen to offer the improved information management support required and permitted by these methods. The methods themselves should bring about a process that permits (without any contractual inhibition), the free flow of information between those who design and those who physically produce buildings. The effective and efficient use of IT should therefore both support and be

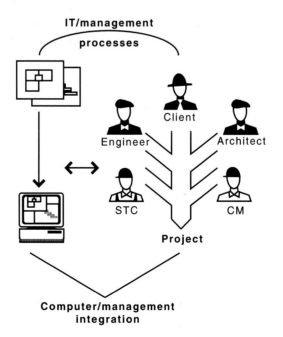

Fig. 1.2 Project procurement and information flow.

supported by the new methods of procurement for building projects.

Research into both Information Technology and project management has to a great extent been mutually supportive in their desired outcome for building project practice. That is to say that for a building project, with regard to cost, it should be reduced; with regard to time it should be faster; and with regard to quality, standards of the finished product should be raised. For each of these outcomes a major requirement is that communication between designers and producers should be improved so that the aims of the former can be understood and realized by the latter.

One key to ensuring that this happens in a timely manner is to realistically evaluate design proposals in terms of construction time, cost and quality standard implications as those proposals are being made.

Joint aims of IT and process research

As these two areas of building research converge and get closer to real practical outcomes in industry, they begin to have some very common aims. For these common aims to be fully realized both the computer-based technological development and the process management must finally satisfy the following needs in building project practice:

☐ to have decision-making models allowing for the impact of design decisions on production and performance-in-use targets for a client's building to be immediately and fully understood;

☐ to have methods of procurement that support a single point of responsibility for the client's project, to provide a greater guarantee that proposed design solutions will be realized within the client's building time and cost targets; and

☐ to have accountability and tracibility through being able to demonstrate and validate design decision-making in order to satisfy quality, environmental and health and safety management requirements.

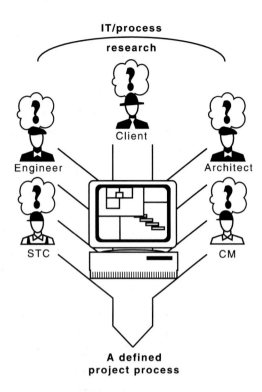

Fig. 1.3 Convergence of IT and project process aims.

In order to satisfy these requirements, a further list must be added in order to make the first viable in terms of ultimate realization:

☐ to have computer-based systems that will directly and interactively link the graphical data of building form to the non-graphical data of building operating performance and resource production;

☐ to have computerized methods of client briefing, architect and engineer designing and construction manager and specialist trade contractor construction designing and managing that reflect and support their usual methods of practice; and

☐ to have simultaneous and concurrent working methods by the various building disciplines (i.e. architects, engineers, construction managers and trade specialists) sharing their particular knowledge in order to arrive at a common solution during the evolution of the client's building project from inception to completion.

In other words, unless both these lists can be fulfilled, the complete basis for building project improvement will not be in place. IT applications must support managed processes and vice versa.

However, once all these wishes have been fulfilled a further opportunity arises regarding the information about a client's building project. That is, having gathered all the information about the product and process of the building project, an integrated model of the building's design, construction and in-use operational factors can be realized. Instead of having separate drawings, schedules, cost data etc. all this graphical and non-graphical information will be grouped in one model and, more importantly, will be related. The most interesting, and potentially most significant, aspect of this situation is that the reasons why various design decisions were agreed and carried out can also be integrated within the information model itself. In other words, the computerized system will be able to represent and present

Fig. 1.4 IT changes to project management.

The building's knowledge base

both the product and the process of the building project throughout its life.

With this potential in mind, some clients already require, as a condition of appointment, that their project teams use computer-based systems for generating and recording the design and construction management information of their projects. The implication and perceived benefits of this approach are not only the efficiency and economy in terms of producing information itself (a major cost in any building project), but also the fact that it will ultimately provide the client with the information means by which the project can be managed.

Therefore, both these main areas of integration research, and their subsequent development in practice, are inevitably leading the construction industry to change the way in which its traditional design and construction disciplines work, and more importantly, how they should work together. The practical implications of this change are dealt with in more detail in Chapters 3 and 4. A fundamental conceptual model that should underpin this change using these new IT and process management approaches is described in the Chapter 2.

Summary

- Basic and applied building research into IT and process management is converging in its aims and desired outcomes.
- IT and process management developments must be mutually supportive if they are to bring about improved building design practice.
- Computer-based systems must be developed to permit shared knowledge between project participants.
- Clients will be able to receive a computerized knowledge base from an integrated information model of their building in the future.

An integrated conceptual model for building projects

The right conceptual view

Models provide us with a way of looking at things in order to understand them. In the building process they can take many forms and provide many different views. It can be argued that drawings themselves are a form of model. So too is a cost plan. The first looks at spatial arrangement, the second at the costs involved. The problems experienced in building design and construction practice have many causes, lack of timely information and co-ordination of everyone's efforts being one of many. Fundamental to these causes is an underlying one of divided knowledge about the total process and product to be realized. The prime cause of this situation and the ways of addressing it practically are dealt with in different ways Chapters 3 and 4. The purpose of this chapter is to address the situation conceptually, because this concerns the way people think about something, and how they think about something will determine their attitudes towards their involvement in any process with which it is concerned. The 'something' in question is of course buildings and their design and construction.

The emergence of the project manager whose existence is now demanded by public clients for all but the smallest of building projects provides a clue to the conceptual issue to be addressed. It can only be assumed that the client's need for a project manager reflects the fact that none of the existing construction professionals appears to be taking such a view on behalf of the client. In other words, nobody is thinking about the project solely from the client's point of view. The architects and engineers are concerned with design, the quantity surveyor (in the UK) is concerned with cost monitoring, the contractor (or more recently the construction manager) is concerned with overall construction and the specialist trade contractor with specific details of construction. All are experts in their own right and make their own contribution, but no-one appears to be concerned with the project as a whole. However, the client is, and unless all project objectives (especially cost and time) are achieved, then the client is not entirely satisfied – even though the building is of a good appearance and performs well in terms of its various structural, services and fabric systems. In addition, if no-one has explicitly, and on the client's behalf, been concerned with the ongoing maintenance and operation of the building when finally constructed, end-user dissatisfaction may also occur.

These disparate views, and the missing client's view, are shown in Fig. 2.1. Such unrelated views, rather than a client's view of a project, support and are continued to be supported by, the traditional method of procurement which conceptually requires that:

☐ methods of production (i.e. the detailed construction processes to be used) are not worked out fully before a price is set;

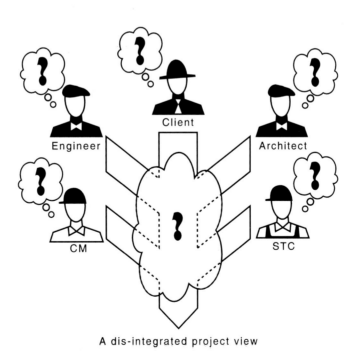

Fig. 2.1 The disparate views of different disciplines.

A dis-integrated project view

☐ the design stage is completed before the actual participants responsible for construction are involved in the project with the result that their particular knowledge has not been applied to the design solution;

☐ the actual participant responsible for production is legally contracted to produce the design (which is why they are called contractors), although they have played no part in the design process itself; and that

☐ the designer (i.e. the architect and/or engineer) has some authority over the producer through the administration of the contract but has no responsibility for the production itself. However, the designer is responsible for providing the production drawings for the construction process and carries a legal responsibility and liability for the constructed end product of the building.

The end result of this conceptual confusion is professional and contractual conflict, which will be dealt with in more detail in Chapter 2. The conceptual confusion itself maintains, and is maintained by, the disparate views. No one conceptual view of the project can be created because it does not yet exist. New project managers merely try to impose one more view on an already disparate set of views. Because such project managers come from one or another of the existing current disciplines, it is likely that their own traditional views will dominate their thinking. Even clients' own project managers have usually started their careers as engineers, quantity surveyors, contractors or architects. Project management education and training may have simply modified these views.

A conceptual view powerful enough to unite the existing disparate views must be one that:

☐ takes into account all the traditional professional and commercial interests that each participant has in the project, for it must be one to which they can all subscribe;

☐ recognizes the nature of building projects in that they begin with a building idea and finish with a building in use, and evolve over time in a series of iterative phases;

☐ supports clear communication between the different project participants that remains consistent over time; and

☐ recognizes the major role of information and the added value it acquires as it is passed between participant and participant, from phase to phase, between the building idea to the building in-use.

In other words any conceptual model must at the same time integrate and address the separate views as well as ensure consistent and clear communication through value added information over the life of the building project, including the maintenance and management of the building in use.

The components and relationships of such an integrated view that a conceptual model should provide and the role of information are shown in Fig. 2.2.

The right process view

Building projects are realized as a result of a process. As complex as practitioners and researchers would like to portray that process, it has, regardless of project size, a fundamental simplicity. That simplicity comes from the fact that, despite the uniqueness of any one building project:

☐ each project participant always contributes the same type of skill and knowledge using the same type of working methods and information representation;

☐ each phase of the project always has the same objectives and the same participant leading that phase; and

☐ each particular contributing participant always leads the same phase and essentially communicates with the other participants from phase to phase with the same type of information representation.

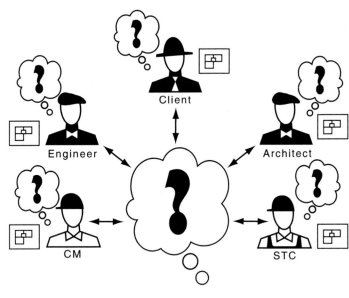

A total project view

Fig. 2.2 An integrated
view for communication
between disciplines.

Based on a standard process model, it is proposed that a building
project needs to be viewed in this way if a chain of conformity to
requirements is to remain unbroken from the inception to the in-
use phases of a client's project. The descriptions used to portray
this building project process model assume that:

☐ the term phase is used instead of stage as the latter implies that
one would be completed before the other began, in practice
they will always overlap with iterations;
☐ every phase would always have a distinct objective and
comprise a basic set of head generic tasks;
☐ the phase overall and the phase tasks in particular could be
described in terms of a standard process model of inputs and
outputs; and
☐ the material input/output of each task in each phase will
always be information and the facilities/equipment will be the
Information Technology (IT) (either on paper or computer-
based).

This interpretation was made because right up to the point of either construction or maintenance when an operative either assembles or disassembles physical building materials and components, each person, even on site, is working with information using methods for its representation and presentation to others.

The standard phase and task process model in which information is the material input and output is shown in Fig. 2.3.

From the point of view of managing quality, it is important to note that any deficiency in any of the inputs to any of the tasks in any of the phases would cause a defective output, which would be defective information. This would in turn cause a deficient information input to other tasks in other phases. How this should be coped with through a quality management methodology is

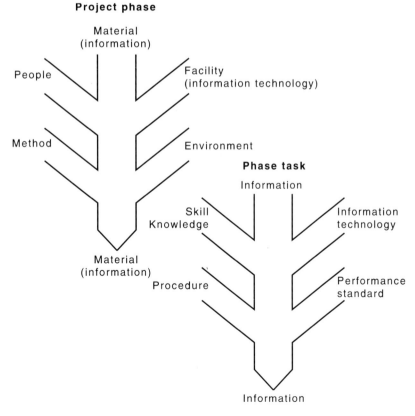

Fig. 2.3 A general model of phases and tasks.

dealt with in detail in *Quality Management for Building Design* (Cornick, 1991).

How a total project can be defined as a series of phases, each with a specific aim that was developed for a total quality management model for building projects is shown in Fig. 2.4. This view of the project process offers major advantages in achieving information integration in that it takes information as the essential linking mechanism between all the tasks and project phases and it requires that the information output of a task is, amongst

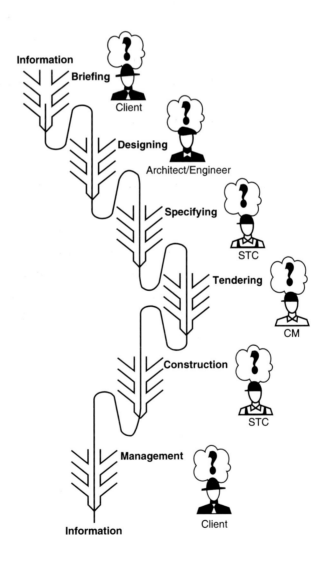

Fig. 2.4 A total quality management model for building projects.

other things, a direct result of the input of a particular participant's knowledge.

This therefore provides the view that the building project
information itself is the means by which each project participant's
knowledge is shared as the building project evolves, passing
iteratively from project phase to project phase. It also stresses the
fact that an equally important input to these tasks is the technology by which the information itself is stored, retrieved, represented, presented and transmitted within and between the tasks
and phases themselves.

This project process view that provides a continuous and
unbroken chain of linked activity tasks therefore provides a
foundation on which to integrate each participant's 'work' as they
'work' with their information by applying their particular knowledge. In order to achieve this effectively, they must actually think,
or conceptualize, together.

Combining a concept/process view for integration

A model for integration must reflect and embody a conceptual
process which allows disparate views to exist but also to combine
to create a common view and one which also has information
transfer as the means by which knowledge is shared. If an
integrated process for building design, construction and operation-in-use is to emerge in practice then:

☐ all project participants must subscribe intellectually to such a
model of how they work together;

☐ the appropriate project environment must be created allowing
such a model view to flourish and be maintained throughout
the life of the project;

☐ the formal methods of binding the participants together and
managing their combined work must not detract from the
model view; and

☐ the IT methods must support knowledge transfer through task information input and output so that value is added as a result of each and every information transfer.

Another view, this time focusing on the diverse activities of the project participants and their information product, can also help towards establishing a sound foundation for integration in practice. The basic generic information products of the combined activities result from the fact that:

☐ the project evolves over time from an outline of the concept through to detail design which will actually be realized by physical production;
☐ the conceptual scheme designed will be represented as building form comprising building element arrangement and material content and finish;
☐ the conceived building form will have to eventually comprise actual building components and materials assembled together (either off- or on-site) in a particular way;
☐ the building component and material assembly will require particular sequences of physical operations in terms of component production and movement through to a final location in a specific building element; and
☐ the final assembly will perform and appear in use in a particular manner implying specific operations for maintenance, repair and demolition.

These aspects can all be considered as the emerging products of the project process in the initial form of briefs, drawings, specifications, schedules, models and then as actual physically-assembled materials, components and elements. Then, finally, in the form of facility information needed to manage and maintain the building in use. There is therefore a combination of information and actual physical products being generated and applied by those who design, construct and ultimately manage a building.

The generic activities carried out by each of the project participants, who use their knowledge to develop and pass information products between each other during the course of the project are as follows:

☐ Clients proclaim a specific need for a project in terms of a site (or an existing building), building type, budget and particular operating requirements for the building in use.

☐ Architects, supported by structural and environmental engineers, propose a particular building form in terms of assembled components and materials in a specific location on the site.

☐ Construction managers propose a plan and programme for physically realizing the proposed building form through off- and on-site assembly in terms of method, material, labour and plant.

☐ Specialist trade contractors often complete detail design and always physically produce, both off- and on-site, the building elements in terms of the assembly of components and materials.

☐ Material/component manufacturers provide the basic materials, components and plant initially in terms of product data and then as the actual product.

☐ Certain external bodies provide guidance and regulations for design and construction performance in terms of standards initially and then through inspection for compliance of either the drawing or construction product.

☐ End-users provide the operational management of the building in terms of activities in the spaces and maintenance of the elements over the life of the building until its final demolition or re-use through conversion.

The building process is therefore also characterized by this underlying product-activity model in which activities can be carried out because the particular participant has a specific knowledge which is manifested in the information product (be it a client's brief, an architect's drawing, a construction manager's programme etc.). Therefore, taking the project as a whole, a production activity, the idea of specific processes being carried out by different participants in a phased manner during the course of a project, can be combined with the idea of each of these processes having continuous information products which are passed backwards and forwards during the course of the project.

The way in which this product-activity model might be considered to operate in the building project process is shown in Fig. 2.5. Features of this model that should be noted are as follows:

- ☐ It is the architect's activity through the generation of the building form information product that provides the means by which all the other project participants' activities and information products can be linked.
- ☐ It is the client's activity through the building brief information product that must take account of the end-users' activity and

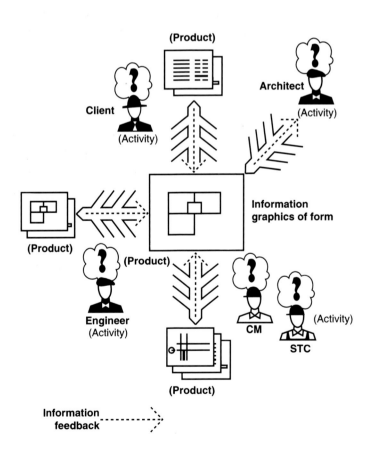

Fig. 2.5 A product activity model for building information.

information product if the building project life-cycle is to be successful.

☐ It is the construction manager's activity through construction plan and programme information which guides and is ultimately dependent upon the specialist trade contractor's activity, in the first instance through detail design and product information and finally through their physical activity and physical building products.

Therefore, a conceptual model, to which all project participants can subscribe, can be defined which recognizes both the nature of a building project over time; the aims and objectives of each of its evolving phases and the activity and information product of each of the participant's work. How such a conceptual model can be supported in practice by methods of procurement and management is described in Chapter 3 and the way in which each project participant can be further encouraged in such a view is developed in Chapter 4.

Summary

■ A strong underlying conceptual model is needed if people are to work together effectively during the course of a building project.

■ The conceptual model can be based on a phase/task model that defines a continuous process chain, linked by information.

■ The conceptual model can also be based on an activity/product model that defines the building project as a series of activities which require information products to be generated and exchanged.

■ Information, both as product and linking mechanism, is fundamental to the conceptual model.

Building
project
procurement
and
management

Procurement method development

New building project procurement methods were introduced into the UK during the 1970s and 1980s with the express aim of overcoming the problems caused by traditional methods. The single biggest problem has been the division in responsibility for the design and construction of a building. This has been identified as a prime cause of building projects being either delayed or beyond budget. Commercial pressure to build even faster and cheaper has helped to accelerate such change. The new methods now account for about 50% of all building project procurement and contracts.

Some 50% of projects still use traditional methods due to the fact that they appear to provide a clear 'lump-sum' price for a designed construction at a particular point in time and clients and the traditional construction disciplines are familiar with this way of working. However, it also generates a number of cost-monitoring and dispute-resolution services that provide work for people! Clients, especially public clients, also feel comfortable with the overall price competition it requires in terms of per-ceived accountability and value for money. The strength of this view has also led to the extension of price competition for the building design services provided by architects and engineers. Although many applied research studies have pointed out the fundamental flaws in the traditional method, only knowledge-able, and particularly private, clients are employing these new methods in practice.

The two essentially distinct methods that have emerged are design and build, in which one participant takes overall respons-ibility for the design and construction process, has a contractual obligation to produce the building for the client and employs specialist trade contractors as sub-contractors; and construction management, which has evolved from management contracting, in which the participant responsible for construction is appointed as a professional consultant equal in status to the architect and engineering consultants and the specialist trade contractors have direct contracts with the client.

Each method can have slight variations in practice depending on the needs of the client, the nature of the project and particular business marketing of any one construction or design organization. The perceived advantages over traditional methods are essentially that:

☐ a building scheme design is completed in the knowledge that the client's cost and time targets can be met because the participant responsible for the construction is involved at the design stage;

☐ the building detail design can be completed within known construction cost and time constraints and simultaneously with the construction planning itself;

☐ the usual disputes (which are usually over untimely information or mis-communication) between separate design and construction organizations are avoided; and

☐ an uninhibited and free flow of information between the design and construction planning and management processes becomes possible.

It is this last benefit that is the most significant for successful computer-integrated building design. If information can flow freely from the output of design processes as an input to the construction planning processes, effective simultaneous designing for the building as an end-product and as a 'construction production system' becomes possible.

The free flow of information in these two methods should become possible because, first, in the design and build method only one organization, be it one firm or a temporary consortium, is contractually and legally responsible for designing and constructing the building; and secondly, in the construction management method, both the organization responsible for designing the building and the organization responsible for managing its construction are considered to have equal consultancy status, providing the client with an equal duty of care.

In both methods there is therefore no contractual or legal inhibition to allowing information to flow backwards and forwards between both processes in a building project. Such inhibition does occur in the traditional method because the architect's and engineer's information (in terms of drawings and specifications) is the contractor's legal document. This still makes architects and engineers wary of sending their information as digital data, even when they have completed the design to be constructed contractually by the contractor.

The way in which the contractual relationship in these three different methods either support or inhibit the free flow of information is shown in Fig. 3.1. The methods of procurement applied to building projects will have either a supporting or detracting effect on whether integration of the processes is

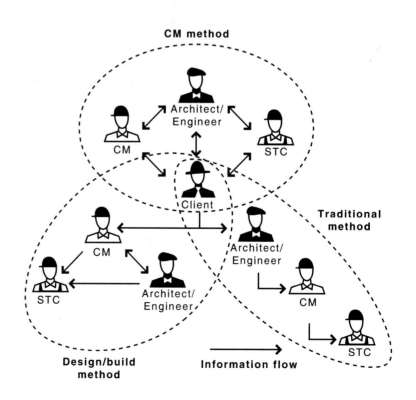

Fig. 3.1 The contractual relationships in methods of procurement.

achieved. Even the actual wording and legal intent of the contracts or agreements used may have such effects. If the processes of the different project participants cannot be positively integrated then knowledge sharing through information exchange will inevitably be inhibited and constrained.

Project-management models

While these new procurement methods have been developing, another concern has arisen over the management of building projects. That is the emergence of a perceived need for project management as a discrete function. Partly coming from the influence of the petro-chemical construction industry and partly because many large clients perceived that their projects were not being managed as a total process and with their best interests at heart, many building projects (down to those of quite small value), have or will soon have project managers. Some are independent of either the designer (architect or engineer) or the constructor (construction manager or specialist trade contractor), having neither direct responsibility for building design or building construction. However, in some cases, both architects and construction managers are responding to this challenge and being either accepted or specifically appointed as the client's project manager also.

In the UK, the two main influences on the emergence of this discipline and paid-for service have been public clients who, on the advice of the UK treasury, should appoint a project manager who, above a certain value of contract, is independent of any of the other design and construction consultants and contractors; and private clients who, lacking building project experience but requiring speed and low costs, feel the need to appoint an independent project manager to ensure that the best value-for-money service is extracted from the design consultants and construction contractors to meet their project needs.

Many large and knowledgeable private clients would see their own in-house staff as providing this project management service.

Much applied research and education and training development has also been addressed to project management in all types of construction in general, and now in building construction in particular. Whether as a recognized discipline to be applied by all project participants or as a new and independent service over and above the traditional design consultants and contractors, project management has emerged as a permanent feature of building projects in the UK.

Project management can be considered as applying at two levels in any building or civil engineering project and is now recognized as such in practice. These are the highest level in the project, where project management is concerned with the overall project in terms of managing all the project participants' contributions towards meeting all the client's needs; and the lower level, where project management is concerned with managing the work of each of the organizations that contribute to the client's project.

Similarities in project management activities exist at both levels, but the prime duty of the project manager is obviously to the client at the highest level and to the individual organization, for example the engineering consultant, at the lower level. New conditions of engagement for the highest level (often referred to as client, total or supra) project management also seem to overlap many duties provided by the traditional consultants, for example cost control, brief development, tendering etc. Traditional design organizations, such as architects and engineers, have also developed these project management services separately from their other design consultancy practices.

The lower level of project management has also been referred to as project co-ordination. However this seems to be more from a need to distinguish it from the higher level of project management than a pure semantic definition of the activities involved. Managing the project is still the aim, even if it is just from a particular project participant's own work and business point of view.

A number of models of construction project management have emerged through international applied research which show

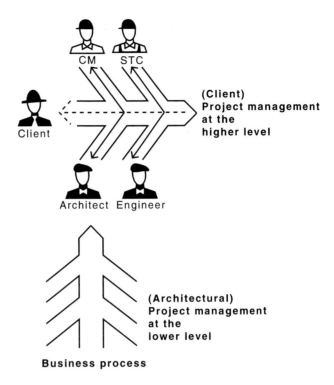

CM   STC

Client

(Client)
Project management
at the
higher level

Architect Engineer

(Architectural)
Project management
at the
lower level

Business process

Fig. 3.2 Project
management at the
higher and lower levels
of a building project.

project-management relationships with other project participants. These, more often than not, demonstrate the difficulties in defining the actual responsibilities of the project manager, when the real responsibilities for design and construction and their direct management still lie with the architects, engineers, main contractors or construction managers and specialist trade contractors who are still carrying out these actual activities. Even in the critical area of design management (that is to say managing the actual scheme and detail design for production itself) there is some confusion as to who, in reality, is effectively managing what!

However, the need to take the project view and to ensure that all the client's needs are being considered (for example the way in which the building as designed and constructed can be funded) is now an accepted and integral part of building project practice. Consequently, managing the briefing, designing, constructing – and even finally the managing/maintaining – phases of the building as a totally integrated process is emerging as both a discrete activity as well as a discipline to be learnt, applied and followed as a particular personal career or business practice. So too, is it becoming both a concern and reality to systematically and precisely project manage to a greater degree, the individual contribution by either architectural or engineering practice involved in the building (or civil engineering) project.

These relationships and levels of application of construction project management are shown in Fig. 3.2. These project management models, and their real application in practice, will gradually and generally influence the way in which building projects are managed as a total process. Whether that management can result in real integration of the design and construction processes by the people responsible being able to work in a simultaneous manner, will depend on other factors.

Project procurement and management for integration

Whenever one more participant is introduced into a process, one of two possible results will occur. On the one hand, the introduction of the independent project manager could provide a means of bringing the designer's and constructor's work together. On the other hand, if the role is simply one that ensures through a reactive old-fashioned command approach and the enforcement of contracts that they should work together, then process integration will not occur as a result of the involvement of this project manager.

Taking lessons from history, even ancient history, the design activity itself should be one that includes the management of the resources required to realize that design. Ensuring that a building's design is one that may be realized within the resources appropriate to the client's needs has historically been the role of the architect. As it is the building's design in terms of its proposed form and materials that will determine the resources required, then design by definition is the lead activity in any building project. Managing the design process is crucial to managing the project, for it is the activity that interprets the client's brief and provides the instructions for the final building, the resources needed for its construction, and how it will perform throughout its life.

In modern building, the evolution of building technology requires that managing the detail design process should take account of a large degree of off-site manufacture. This is obviously more true the larger the project and the more complex the architectural design. In this sort of situation, it is obviously important that the detail design of the specialist trade contractor who actually produces and installs the building element, for example a large spanning roof, is managed in parallel with the architect's and engineer's building design process. The methods and principles of doing this are well understood by architects, engineers and the professional construction managers who can also make the link to the construction process on site. It is difficult to see how another role, that is to say of the independent project manager, is needed to support and improve this type of design integration.

However, it is not difficult to see how these methods and principles can be transferred down in scale and apply to even the smallest building project. This is because any building is created by specialists producing, installing and constructing, in other words assembling the individual building elements off and on site. Only the scale differs between projects and that is a direct relationship between size and complexity of element and size and complexity of specialist organization. A small simple element may only need one specialist operative to design the detail, produce and install, but the method and principle of managing the design integration will be the same. The essential objective is to ensure that the detail design of the specialist for production and installation of the building element will also satisfy the architect's or engineer's building scheme design in terms of the appearance and performance of that element when it is finally in place and in use. It is in fact the only way to ensure that the scheme design as proposed can also meet the client's cost and time targets for construction while simultaneously meeting the appearance and performance targets determined by the architect and engineer.

This is due to the fact that it is the specialist, individual or organization, who will actually expend the resources, in terms of labour, material and equipment, who will spend the money and take the time to realize any particular building element. The fee and time required by the architect and engineer to design and co-ordinate the detail design and the fee and time required by the construction manager to plan, co-ordinate and control the production, installation and construction by the specialists, accounts for the remainder of the cost and time of the client's building project.

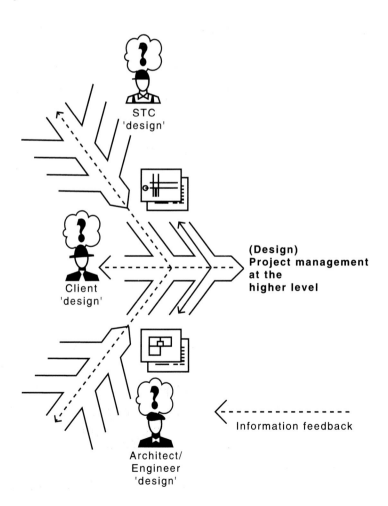

Fig. 3.3 The relationships and objectives of scheme design and detail design for production management.

The relationships and objectives necessary in managing the essential design activity of a project are shown in Fig. 3.3.

The aim of any project management, at either level but in particular at the highest level, should therefore be primarily to support the integration of the specialist trade contractor's detail design for a production process with the architect's and engineer's scheme for a detail design process. If cost and time, as well as quality, are also to be controlled and assured, then both design processes must also be integrated with the production and construction planning process. The method of procurement must also allow this integration to happen without hindrance.

New project organization for integration

It is not only the construction industry that is endeavouring to improve the integration of its design and production processes. The manufacturing industries in the UK now wish to a great extent to overlap their product design and production design processes. Their aim is firstly to avoid expensive re-design of a product when they get to the production stage in order to make themselves more competitive, and secondly, to reduce the amount of time necessary from a new idea for a product to the point at which the product is eventually on sale in the market place, with the potential to beat the competition.

Similarities between the aims of the modern construction client and the need for the construction industry to respond to this demand are obvious. What is not so obvious is that in order to meet these requirements, the manufacturing industries are having to reorganize themselves into flexible and dynamic project teams, something the construction industry has always done! However, the methods of their reorganization, known as business process re-engineering, do include some concepts which could be offered to the construction industry. These new approaches to manufacturing production and business re-engineering suggest that the new organization should, among other things, focus activities on the material and information flow of the core process for which that organization exists. The purpose of this focus is to ensure that material and information flow is controlled for minimal variability and cycle time and continuous improvement with respect to waste and value.

Technology, including Information Technology (IT), is seen to be the enabling tool that brings about efficiency for this 'flow process control'. The theme is again one of stressing the importance of information which is relevant to the product being able to flow freely and as efficiently and economically as possible throughout the process. It is also one which emphasizes the importance of adding value to, and minimizing waste of, information as it passes through the process. IT should serve that end and that end only. The key to success is to use information in a way that maximizes its added value and mimimizes its waste at every exchange in the process of production.

In the case of building production, the organization in question is the project organization which is temporal and initially formed by the way in which the client procures the services of the other project participants. The method of project management at the higher level will determine how this organization operates. The core process of this organization is to produce a building, that is:

☐ the site, budget and brief which is determined by the client;
☐ the overall form and material which is defined by the architect and engineers; and
☐ the actual physical material realization which is produced by the specialist trade contractors using the products of component manufacturers as a result of the planning and control by the construction manager.

If these new re-engineered organizational approaches to achieve integration are to be adopted by the construction industry as a response to the pressures from powerful clients, then a radical view should be taken of future project procurement and project-management methods. This means even questioning the new building project procurement and management methods previously described in this chapter. The most ideal procurement method would be one in which the project organization ranks the client and all other participants as equal partners. This would enable each to contribute to the evolving information about the proposed building as soon as their expert knowledge was required. Thus, information could be given and received with the maximum added value and minimum waste, as it would be for the purposes of honest communication rather than to enforce, react to or dispute contractual conditions.

In the light of this ideal, the worst approach must be the traditional method and the best approach, the construction management method. Design and build, although integrating the design and construction management processes, still excludes the client and specialist trade contractors from the organization by retaining the latter as sub-contractors. It may also exclude external architects and engineers also retaining them as sub-contractors. The introduction of the independent project manager over any of these existing methods does not of itself bring about the required new project organization. The new independent project manager can still preside, and more often than not does,

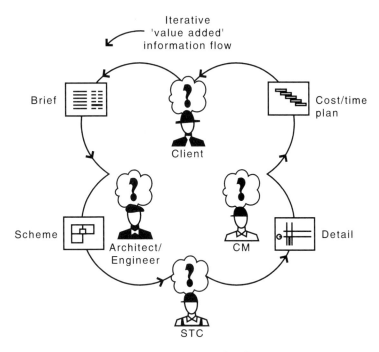

Fig. 3.4 Old to new project organizations.

New project organization

over these procurement methods without creating the new project organization.

How these new project organizations should enable information passing and exchange to share the knowledge of equal-status partners is shown in Fig. 3.4.

So, if new forms of project organization that support efficient and economic information integration in the production of buildings are to be adopted, the methods of project procurement, contracts and management must, at the very least, encourage and support the notion of equal partnership. This is turn will foster honest communication, a prerequisite for uninhibited and timely information flow, that must be the basis of control that minimizes variability, cycle time and waste and maximizes added value in the flow of information.

Once these features are all in place within the building project organization then, and only then, can computer-based systems be developed and applied for continuous improvement of information flow and integration. The way in which a concept of architectural, engineering and construction design can play a major role in these new project organizations, as well as being the spur for the integration of information technologies in building, is developed in the next chapter.

Summary

- Forms of procurement can either inhibit or support the free flow of information between all project participants.
- Design and build and construction management methods are contractually the least inhibiting.
- Project management is a discipline and activity that causes a total project view to be taken to ensure that all the client's needs are met.
- New project organizations will require and support the maximum added value and minimum waste of information flowing through the building project process.
- IT is seen to be the essential enabling tool for the passage of information.

Architectural, engineering and construction design

Design in building

Designing in the building process has always been considered to be an activity carried out by architects and engineers. This is because they are the professions who propose the end-product of the building process, that is to say, the building's form and material fabric, supporting structure and environmental controlling services. Distinctions between architectural design and engineering design have also been made, the former being focused more on the aesthetic appearance of a building, and the latter on its structural and environmental performance. Recently, even UK quantity surveyors have been arguing for the title of designer, as under the traditional method of procurement they often have a cost, and sometimes specification, input to the project information.

Architectural design has mainly become associated with the activity of satisfying the aesthetic, social and spatial criteria for buildings. It is expected to be the activity that ensures that building legislation and good practice standards are complied with, as well as the technical performance of the building's fabric. Structural engineering design may also be considered to concern itself with aesthetic appearance, as the structure becomes an essential architectural feature of the proposed building. Both architectural and engineering design can involve the use of either prescriptive or performance specifications which instruct specialist trade contractors on how technically to detail design the component assembly of a particular building element. In the latter case, all the technical detail design is left to the specialist trade contractor to meet a given aesthetic and operational performance. Generally, the term design is currently ascribed to the activities of architects, engineers and, in part and because they actually make and install a building element, the specialist trade contractors. Over the last few centuries, in many people's minds, design by architects has also become associated simply with being concerned with aesthetic and social concepts of building. Problems in maintaining the client's cost and time budgets are then cited as the result of architectural designs not being practical when it comes to the actual construction of the building itself. In the building process, design has therefore become disassociated from construction as an activity, but is in need of management if the resulting construction process is to be cost- and time-effective and produced to the expected quality standard.

Architectural design has therefore become the activity that precedes all other building design activity and actual construction. Consequently, when actual construction is considered with the aim of achieving the client's cost and time targets, some re-design may have to be carried out. Re-design, for the purposes of production then occurs and architects carry the blame for not designing correctly in the first instance!

The re-design more often than not means changing fabric or services detail, either the specified components and finishes or the way in which they are to be assembled, for it is impractical at this stage in the project to alter the overall building form and structure. However, much evidence suggests that when the overall building form, fabric and structure itself are determined, so are the likely achievable cost, time and standard of construction. This is because all the environmental services, which now account for a high proportion of building costs, have to be designed to suit the building's form and fabric.

The building's form, fabric and structure also dictate how the whole building and its components can be assembled, which in turn ultimately determines construction cost and time.

A further problem associated with architectural design is that the actual operational use of the proposed building has not been clearly thought through and defined in explicit detail in the client's brief. The result is that once the building does come into operation as a facility it is seen in some ways as being inadequate to the end-user, who may or may not have been the commissioning client in the first instance. In this situation there has been a tendency for architects to blame clients for not knowing what they want or clients to blame architects for not fully understanding their, and their end-user's, building needs. The fact that re-design, which by now becomes remodelling, immediately occurs could be considered a failure in the communication of the actual building requirements in the first case. Later remodelling may be perfectly understandable as a consequence of changing operational needs.

How then can these current deficiencies in the design process be overcome and what role does the integration of information have to play?

A new approach to designing for building

If the activity of design can be described as one of initiating change in man-made things or planning change or rational decision-making, then it could be argued that all the participants involved in a building are designers. When clients formulate an initial brief they are implicitly proposing that something about their business needs to be changed, whether that business is concerned with manufacturing products or providing a service such as care or education. For example, a change, be it for improvement or expansion or both, in the business's operating activity is perceived to be needed which requires a new or altered building space. If the client's business is property development itself, then the purpose of the building space becomes the making of money out of the identified building needs of other end-users. In one sense a brief could be said to be a design itself and the client a designer for building 'in-use operation'. Similarly, construction managers, when they formulate a construction plan for production, could be said to be planning changes in the state of materials, manpower and plant in order for these resources to come together physically to realize new or altered enclosed building spaces. So they too could be said to be designers for building production, especially if the form of procurement provides for their involvement as the scheme design is being proposed by the architect and engineers.

Both client and construction manager have in mind cost, time and a standard of building finish and performance factors to which their designs will be related. In the case of the client these factors are a desirable limit for both first and on-going running costs of in-use operation; in the case of the construction manager these factors are a predictable limit based on the judged resources needed for production. The architect's, engineer's and specialist contractor's designs are then proposed, building form and element solutions which should match the solutions designed by the client and construction manager. The purpose of the matching should be to ensure that all the desirable cost, time, standard and performance factors can be confidently predicted in a commonly agreed solution. The process of matching will be to integrate everyone's designing activity.

'Designing for production' is already becoming an accepted concept in building practice. It is taken to mean that the architectural and engineering design will also have taken account of detailed production implications in what is proposed. This will be because the designer, presumably the architect or engineer, will also have been able to have considered an economic and efficient assembly process as well as the final assembly in designing a building form or element. This approach is now even more important with the advent of the EU Construction Design and Management (CDM) Regulations. These require that site safety of the operative should be analysed for risk by the designer at the design stage and passed on as information to contractors tendering and planning for the construction phase of the building project. This means that architectural, engineering and any subsequent specialist contractor design must now take certain account of the production factors of the required subsequent construction. In effect, production design for construction is becoming a necessity in order to satisfy, in the first instance, newly imposed legislation to ensure the health and safety of site operatives.

'Designing for operation', that which the client would have to do for the required building as a facility, is not such an obvious concept in practice. At least not for most buildings, although in the case of a process plant it is more recognized. This is because in a process plant the 'operation' purpose of the facility for which the engineering design is carried out is virtually the built facility itself. In buildings, this may not be so obvious. However, a rigorous user study of the intended building use which is more than simply a list of accommodation, but describes the purposes and processes to be undertaken by the user, may go some way towards a concept of 'designing for operation' by clients themselves, for it is only the client who in the end can know the real purpose for which the new or altered building is intended. In addition, it is only the client who can make priority choices about an evolving building solution when the inevitable trade-offs arise in criteria satisfaction that will ultimately affect the in-use operation.

All project participants could then be considered to have the status of designer, each having a distinct design responsibility to create the same product solution, that is to say the building. With this view, they are all in once sense, equal.

Architectural, engineering, construction and operation design as knowledge sharing

If the above equal status as designers can be accepted by all the project participants, then each one's actions and activities should follow a design process. If design can be accepted as 'the conceptualization of changing states of being' in a building project, then each and every participant has to carry out that process in order to make their contribution to the project. This means that each of the project participants must, in the first instance, conceptualize, and then think rationally about those concepts, with regard to their own particular interest in the evolving building solution, in that:

☐ the client has to conceptualize and think rationally about how the proposed building as a managed and maintained facility will support the desired change in the end-user's specific activity operations and general well-being, as well as their desired cost, time, standard and performance limits;

☐ the architect has to conceptualize and think rationally about how the proposed building's form and material will bring about change in the existing built and natural environment in order to support the client's managed and maintained facility;

☐ the structural and services engineers have to conceptualize and think rationally about how their structural and environmental systems will serve the building's form and material as a support to the client's managed and maintained facility;

☐ the specialist trade contractors have to conceptualize and think rationally about how the proposed building will bring about change in resources to produce their particular element or system as part of the building's form and material; and

☐ the construction manager has to conceptualize and think rationally about how the proposed building's form and material will bring about change in resources to produce all the building elements.

Having established both their status and work as co-designers there will be an order and relationship about their work in considering the proposed building solution. Their co-designing work will be in the form of a knowledge contribution from each of them based on their particular experience and expertise. Their method of working together will therefore be in the form of knowledge sharing in order to evolve a commonly agreed building solution. However, as all their knowledge will have to be brought to bear on a proposed building form and material sooner, rather than later, there will have to be an order to their relationship. For example, a suggested building form and material conceived by the architect will allow the client, construction manager and specialist trade contractor to conceive their own designed solution. However, this process must occur from the

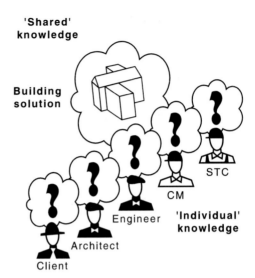

'Shared' knowledge

Building solution

STC

CM

Engineer

'Individual' knowledge

Architect

Client

Fig. 4.1 The order and relationship of 'design' knowledge contributions.

outset of the project and, if the solution is to be a truly co-designed solution, the architect's conceived solution should only progress as and when all the others have agreed conceptually. The order and relationship of their conceptions are shown in Fig. 4.1.

The contribution of each participant's knowledge as co-designer, starting with the client, means that the evolving building solution is conceptually agreed by all, rather than being one participant's concept (i.e. the architect's) to which all others have to subscribe. However, the necessary order of knowledge application means that architect's contribution is pivotal, in that all the other participants' knowledge can only be meaningfully shared when it has been applied to the project by suggesting the form and material. The logical reason for this is that unless this is done first there is nothing in building terms to which the client's, engineer's, specialist trade contractor's or construction manager's knowledge can be conceptually applied. A comparable situation will be seen to be true in the manufacturing industries, as described in Chapter 5.

Architectural, engineering, construction and operation design – information exchange

Knowledge sharing by each of the co-designers can only occur practically if they can exchange design information which will represent the output from and input to their individual knowledge contribution. Information exchange methods will therefore have to ensure that information generated and transmitted is:

☐ a true reflection of the nature of change to be brought about by the individual designer, for example an activity operation from the client; and

☐ a useful representation of the input that the particular designer is making from their specific knowledge domain and a meaningful presentation as an output to each and every other particular designer involved in the building project.

The collective conceptualization of an agreed building solution can only come about through a series of iterations in which information value is added at each transfer of the knowledge contribution from each of the co-designers. The knowledge of each designer has to be represented, presented and exchanged in order that information value is added at each pass as follows:

☐ From the client – the general building facility performance requirements of a particular business or activity process with regard to its operations and the situation of the building site and project programme and cost.

☐ From the architect – aesthetic appearances which are a result of the shape, proportions, arrangements, material colour and texture of building elements brought together in an overall building form; spatial arrangements of building enclosures which have to serve specific activities and relationships of future building users with regard to their size, shape and arrangement; the spatial and aesthetic features of building forms and how they relate to their located site and wider surrounding environment; the general technical performance requirements for building fabric, structural and services elements and enclosures with regard to their structural stability, environmental performance and a range of other factors that all contribute to the health, safety and comfort of the building's end-users; the general technical production requirements for the assembly of building elements off and on site to form enclosures with regard to their material content, size, shape and arrangement and the situation of the building site and project programme.

☐ From the engineers – the particular technical performance requirements of the structural elements, both above and below ground, with regard to the safe transmission of building loadings; the particular technical performance requirements of the service elements, both above and below ground, with regard to the provision of a healthy, safe and comfortable building environment; the general technical production requirements of the assembly of the building structure and services, both off and on site with regard to their material content, size, shape and arrangement and the situation of the building site and project programme.

(Both architects and engineers have a general understanding of building design legislation, good practice design guidance and manufactured building products, all of which is needed to support their design activity and all of which requires constant updating. Both also have a general construction cost understanding of the building elements and enclosures they deal with, although this knowledge has resided with quantity surveyors in the UK and other UK-influenced countries.)

☐ From the specialist trade contractor – the particular technical performance requirements of a specific building element with regard to its appearance and function and relation to adjoining elements; the particular technical production requirements for the assembly of a specific building element, both off and on site, with regard to its material content, size, shape and arrangement and the situation of the building site and project programme.

☐ From the construction manager – the general technical production requirements of whole buildings with regard to the assembly of all building elements, the situation of the building site and overall cost and time programmes.

How the architect's information about the evolving building's 'form and material' needs to be represented and presented in transmission and translation so that each of the other co-designer's own knowledge framework can be applied is shown in Figs. 4.2–4.4:

☐ for the client as building operation designer: Fig. 4.2;
☐ for the architect and engineers as building 'form, structure and environment' designers, but in this instance as feedback to themselves: Fig. 4.3;
☐ for the specialist trade contractors and construction managers as building 'production' designers: Fig. 4.4.

Based on the architect's graphical representation of the emerging building form and material, each designer should able to visualize the information representation in order to relate it to their applied knowledge area. The client 'sees' in terms of textually-described activity processes and relationships and

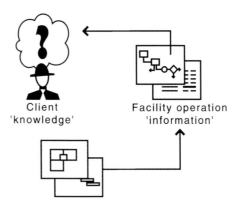

Fig. 4.2 Client knowledge representation as building 'operation' design information.

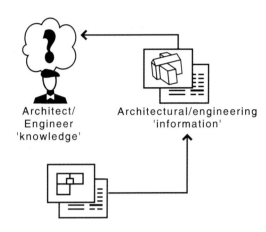

Fig. 4.3 Architect–engineer knowledge representation as building 'form, structure and environment' design information.

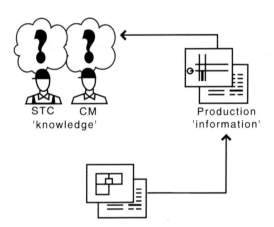

Fig. 4.4 Specialist trade contractors – construction manager knowledge representation as building 'production' design information.

numerically-described cost and time accounting – in other words alpha-numeric data.

The architect 'sees' in terms of graphically-described building spatial arrangement, element enclosure and material finish and textually-described material content – in other words graphical/alpha-numeric data. The engineer 'sees' in graphically-described structural and services systems and materials and numerically-described supporting calculations – in other words graphical/alpha-numeric data. The specialist trade contractor 'sees' in terms of graphically-described component assembly supported by numerically-described resource use – in other words graphical/alpha-numeric data. The construction manager 'sees' in terms of textually-described activities and numerically-described resource use – in other words alpha-numeric data.

If these co-designers are to design simultaneously, so that the impact of anyone's information output can immediately be taken as another's input for knowledge application, then it must be useful for common information visualizations to be made. In other words, they can all see the same building information from their own point of view.

Architectural, engineering, construction and operation design – computer applications for shared knowledge information exchange

The development of CAD computer-based systems for architecture, engineering and construction by software suppliers has essentially been driven by the need to provide their customers with drawing applications. In other words, to represent and present a whole or part of a building form and material in either a 2D or 3D mode. The generation, alteration and presentation of graphical data by architects, engineers and specialist trade contractors is more convenient and possible at far greater speeds than by previous manual methods.

Other computer-based systems, which can be CAD-related, also help architects, engineers, specialist trade contractors and construction managers to generate, alter and present a range of alpha-numeric data, for example, specifications, cost and component schedules, time programmes etc. The simultaneous generation of graphical and alpha-numeric data with simple information exchange is also possible, even with comparatively low-cost systems, (for example, the automatic generation of the alpha-numeric data of component assembly quantity and cost from the generation of the graphical data of a proposed building's 'form and material'). This capability could allow, at a broad level, information exchange between architect and construction manager – or even the direct transfer to specialist trade contractors.

However, the sharing of knowledge through computer-based information exchange methods requires much more than the simple geometric graphical and alpha-numeric data exchange described above. The methods must allow the development of an internalized common image by each co-designer. They must all 'see' an information outcome at any stage in the evolution of the building solution, to which they can immediately apply their particular knowledge.

Simultaneous with the architect generating the CAD geometric graphical data of a conceived building's 'form and material':

☐ the client's computer-based application should ideally present a managed and maintained facility system;
☐ the engineer's computer-based application should ideally present a structural or environmental system;
☐ the specialist trade contractor's computer-based application should ideally present a particular element component assembly resource and performance system; and
☐ the construction manager's computer-based application should ideally present an all-element assembly resources system.

Ideally, each application should present common cost, time and quality standard consequences so that all can concurrently understand how the client's expected targets are in fact being met as the building design solution evolves. It is only in this way that everyone can be assured that as design decisions are being made, the resulting solution is meeting all identified requirements for the building project. This can only occur if all project participants can think in parallel. Unless shared knowledge and common conceptual models are allowed by computer-based information exchange methods, they will offer no advantage over former paper-based methods for simultaneous designing. Conversely, unless the current CAD-related systems (described in Chapter 6), and the near-future integrating tools and techniques (described in Chapter 7), are applied (a) with the right conceptual building project process view by all the project participants (as described in

Chapter 2), and (b) within the supportive building project procurement methods which allow all project participants to work together described in (as described in Chapter 3), their potential for information exchange will not be fully realized.

Summary

- Design as an activity should be undertaken by all the project participants if a commonly conceived and agreed solution to a building project is to be realized.
- Clients should 'design for operation' and construction managers should 'design for production' in parallel with the architect's, engineer's and specialist contractor's design activity.
- Information exchange in the building project process must be a means of sharing knowledge through appropriate representation and presentation of the emerging building solution.
- CAD-related computer-based applications must support these ends if integrated design is to become a reality.

Computer-
integrated
design
and
manufacture
in
another
industry

Why compare the construction industry's processes with those of the manufacturing industry?

In the 1960s it was fashionable to compare the production of buildings with the production of motor cars. Writings and illustrations from that period would even make a visual comparison of the external appearance of the two. Having their stylistic roots in the 1930s view and prediction of machine-age architecture, the system building of the 1960s, in particular public housing, took on the appearance of 'industrial production' in their final building product. In fact, apart from the prefabricated concrete cladding panels, very little else was produced in a factory. The costs were in the end no less and the appearance and performance of the resulting building were unsatisfactory and ultimately rejected. Later production methods for building that emerged in the 1970s and 1980s, such as prefabricated trussed rafters, glazed cladding panels, toilet 'pods' etc., have all been applied to buildings that architecturally have a 'non-system' appearance in comparison with those built in the 1960s.

However, for the purposes of describing the potential of integrated CAD in buildings, a comparison with how it is likely to be applied in the automotive industry is useful. This is due to the similarities in both the product and the process of each man-made object. With regard to the product, both car and building:

☐ enclose space to be used for both in-use operation and maintenance;
☐ have an overall appearance dictated by aesthetic fashion and a perceived visual acceptance by the end-user; and
☐ comprise component parts of structure, fabric and services systems.

With regard to their process of design and production, the similarities are that:

☐ one set of designers conceives the overall form of the product and how all its parts would fit and work together;
☐ other designers conceive how all the system parts can be engineered as an overall assembly (these could be compared to the architects and engineers of the construction industry) for which,
☐ other production designers conceive how the component parts determined by the first two sets of designers and supplied by other organizations, can be assembled physically to complete the finished product. (These could be compared to construction managers, however the specialist trade contractor as assembler of the component parts within the final product has no equivalent – this is done by the product manufacturer himself.)

In both the automotive and construction industries the final product has to satisfy through its appearance and performance in use in order to meet the needs of a customer. In the automotive industry, this customer is the car-buying public whose perceived needs have been determined by the automotive manufacturing company's marketing department. In rare circumstances, the customer may be an individual client. In the construction industry, the ultimate customer of the building product is the end-user whose perceived needs are determined by the commissioning client. End-product quality standards, capital cost and production time, are determined and controlled by the car-manufacturing company in the automotive industry. In the construction industry, things are not quite so clear cut. Although the commissioning client may set targets for quality, cost and time criteria, it is the architects and engineers as designers and the construction managers and specialist trade contractors constructing that design who together control and determine whether they are finally achieved. Although the methods of building procurement may divide these responsibilities, the functions and objectives are the same.

This means that any computer-based CAD-related approaches being developed to support the manufacture of motor cars can be considered equally relevant to the production of buildings. The same generic type of information needs to be related and integrated, throughout the design processes that precede the physical production process. This to represent and present overall product form and arrangement of non-standard and standard physical parts through the use of 3D and 2D graphical data which has performance and production analysis values, from predetermined rules through the use of alpha-numeric textual data.

This fact is recognized by CAD vendors whose CAD systems can be used equally to model car and car component forms and building and building component forms, using the same basic computer technology. The CAD-related systems that are used to demonstrate how a driver or mechanic can fit into the cab or work under the bonnet of a car are the same as those that can 'walk thru' a building user inside an enclosed space. The computer-based systems, either indirectly or directly related to the CAD-generated files that can structurally analyse a car component for stress, are the same generic systems as those that analyse a building's structural frame. Equally those systems that deal with production-activity duration and sequence and associated costs in building construction can deal with similar functions in car manufacture. Although the final product of car and building may differ significantly in terms of scale, location, form and material, as may the process in terms of single and multiple participating organizations, the fundamental way in which the product is realized through an evolutionary process is, with minor exceptions, identical. Such exceptions relate merely to the way in which the product is procured rather than to the functions and objectives involved. That the automotive industry prototypes and then mass produces, whereas the construction industry tends to virtually build its prototypes, does not alter the fact that the

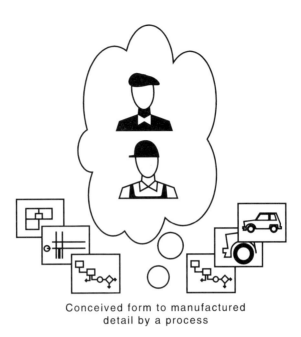

Conceived form to manufactured
detail by a process

Fig. 5.1 Comparison
between car and
building design and
production.

design process activity that precedes production is nonetheless
the same.

The drive towards simultaneous engineering in the automotive industry

This comparison between the two industries can be taken even
further by looking at the way in which they are each currently
responding to their respective markets. In the construction industry the pressure has been to reduce the time between the
client's initial brief and a building being ready for occupation and
use. This was particularly important during the boom in construction of commercial properties during the 1980s, in order to obtain
return on investment as soon as possible. Other types of industrial
and service buildings also require this reduction in time in order
to meet rapidly changing social, economical and political needs.
Demand for higher standards of quality in a finished building has
now added to this pressure for reduced time and lower costs. In

the automotive industry, there is now a need to get from the 'new product idea' to the 'product being available in the market place' as soon as possible for competitive reasons. In both industries there is a need to constantly reduce costs as well as meet ever-increasing improvements in the quality standard of the finished product – for the car and building end-user.

In the automotive industry, as in other manufacturing industries, the means of meeting these demands have been through the evolution of simultaneous or concurrent engineering. (The difference between the two terms is merely one of two slightly different methodological ideas.) In the car-manufacturing industry, simultaneous engineering means overlapping the activities of designing the end-product with the activities of designing the production for the new model of the car. Concurrent engineering is the use of multi-functional teams within one company representing manufacturing, purchasing, finance and marketing during the design process. Essentially, this reduces the overall design time and eliminates costly re-designs of a product when the design proposal then has to be considered for production. The primary method applied in order to achieve this has been a reorganization of the way in which the different 'designers' carry out their work, rather than through the specific application of computer-based systems. By placing production engineers (i.e. those who design for production) in teams with the stylists and packagers (i.e. those who design the end-product) it is hoped that end-product design will simultaneously meet the production design requirements as it evolves. The design analysts, who assess the various car components for a range of performances in use, would then make their contributions to the integrated design as and when appropriate during the various stages of the integrated design process. Partnering with preferred sub-contractors for the manufacture and supply of specialist parts on a long-term basis also allows them to make detail design contributions at appropriate points in the design process.

A comparison of the organizational aspect of simultaneous engineering shows some interesting similarities in both industries. The fact that building design and production is always carried out in project teams and, with the design and build and construction management methods, uses construction advice during design means the mapping can be shown, as in Fig. 5.2.

CAD-related applications for integration in the automotive and aerospace industries

Just as in building design, CAD is used for the 3D geometric modelling of the product form. Stylists can create a car shape for all-round external and internal visualization with animated 3D CAD. With further surface shading and photorealism systems, both car and building material and form can be visually modelled for near-realistic appearances. The packagers can then visualize

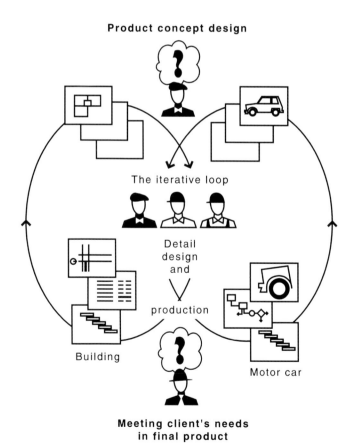

Fig. 5.2 Simultaneous engineering – designing for product and production in car manufacture.

and measure how the components can be assembled into the car body form, also using 3D solid geometric modelling and possibly animation. Even more sophisticated 3D animated geometric modelling can be carried out by visualizing how human users can ergonomically use the inside as drivers and passengers. They can also consider how the spaces between working component parts within engine compartments will allow for future in-use maintenance of human maintenance engineers working within such spaces. This type of application has been effectively applied most recently not in the automotive but in the aerospace industry. Using an advanced CAD modelling system called Catia, the Boeing designers and builders have been able to extensively model their new 777 airliner for a range of production and in-use performance requirements. This system also has the capability of carrying out calculating analysis for weight and stress direct from the 3D model files.

In automotive manufacturing, the CAD-related graphics systems that model forms and assembled forms are still only generally used to visualize shape arrangement and transfer geometric data, indirectly, to other computer-based systems that deal with performance-in-use calculated analysis, (for example, structurally and thermally applied loads, crash/ride/handling characteristics, and how components interact with regard to noise and vibration). The CAD-related applications in automotive design, however, are still not that integrated in terms of direct information exchange. FEA, or finite element analysis, packages can either operate within the same operating environment as CAD or use transferred geometric files. CAD 'solid' modelling systems are useful for such things as designing and structurally analysing engine block components. CAD 'surfacing' modelling systems provide realistic visualization for the stylists and can also generate input files for FEA systems.

The development of Knowledge-based Engineering (KBE) systems, which originated within the Artificial Intelligence (AI) field of computer science in the automotive industry, has provided opportunities to 'model knowledge' of various aspects of automotive design. ICAD, a commercially-available KBE system, has

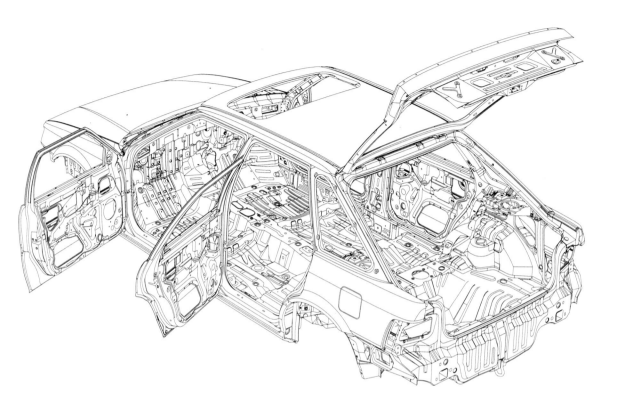

Fig. 5.3 CAD-generated car body form and component parts.

been used to create overall car design concepts by generating car forms according to pre-defined rules of exterior and interior shape and arrangement. Similarly, the same system can be used to generate car 'detail parts' according to pre-defined rules of particular component assemblies. The value of using and degree of application of such new CAD-related computer-based systems in automotive design lies in the capability of all AI-based applications to encapsulate experiential rules so that they can be used to generate or validate solutions.

The ICAD system, and others that will surely follow in its place, allows designers the freedom to concentrate on creative and innovative designs because such systems can deal with all the vital performance criteria that any solution must satisfy. For example, the ICAD 'manikin' can embody the 'intelligence' to ensure that the simulation of such things as visibility from within a car meet the minimum legal requirements. The placement of such things that particular components have to function for, such as windscreen wiped area and headlight beam direction, can also be verified by this type of system. The basis of the technology of these systems is that they understand the drawn objects as product models to which a range of attributes can be ascribed. These objects can then interact with other objects within the computer so that the impact of one thing upon another can be

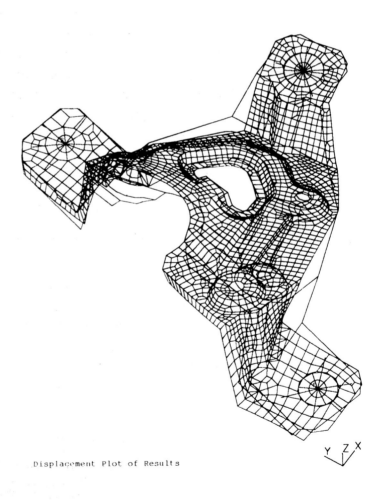

Fig. 5.4 Computer-generated stress analysis of form and parts.

understood and analysed, such as the relationship between the steering wheel and windscreen as viewed by the 'manikin'.

The future for such systems is still being debated in the automotive industry: to actually generate design solutions or verify and validate design solutions generated by human designers? However, the future of these types of advanced systems is assured in one way or another because, in spite of their very high initial and data inputting costs, the time they save in routine calculation and re-calculation is time they save in the design process.

These advanced systems are important in the manufacture of any product – car or building – in that they also offer the potential to store and retrieve information used to make design decisions. The specific areas of knowledge used in either overall form or particular detail design can be encapsulated in the computer-based system and applied from project to project. This means that design lessons learnt on one project can be applied on another and new designs can be based on systematic improvement of existing design solutions. It also means that the reasons for any design decision can be recorded, demonstrated and agreed by all those involved in project.

The client's expectation of the construction industry

Clients, especially industrial clients, may have an expectation that the CAD-related tools and techniques they are using to create their own products will be utilized by the construction industry to create new plants and facilities – that is, to create the construction industry's 'product'. Industrial clients see their new buildings as plants which are to become an integral part of the manufacturing process used to produce their products. This plant must be a direct support to the economic and efficient operation of the manufacturing process. This will also be true of commercial clients who offer a service rather than make a product and see their building as a facility. Even clients who are operating traditional people-centred services, such as health care or education, must increasingly see their buildings as a very direct support to the economic and efficient provision of their service. If CAD-related, or other computer-based, tools and techniques are seen as a beneficial support to the client's production or service process, there will be a natural expectation that they will also be beneficial in the design and production of the client's building. This is particularly so if their use improves the communication of the client's building needs to the architect as the design is being developed. In all cases and with all types of client, the dimensional, material and performance information that is generated by the building design as it develops needs to be integrated and reviewed for consistency with the information generated by the design of the process to be enclosed by the building.

This may be difficult to appreciate and actually apply in the case of buildings that become a facility for clients who operate a commercial or people-centred service. (One attempt to do so is described in Chapter 8.) It is far more evident when the building being designed is to be a plant to enclose a clearly understood and defined manufacturing process for a product – for example a motor car.

Therefore, the ability to interact with designers and construction managers (who may still be separate general contractors and quantity surveyors) during the building design development phase of a project is becoming highly desirable for particular industrial clients. This is to ensure that the finished building, as a plant, will be fully integrated with their own production equipment, which together comprise their own manufacturing process, without any costly re-design and/or reconstruction during the subsequent construction and managing/maintainence-in-use phases of the building project. One example is the use of a 'partnering' project management method between an automotive manufacturer, an architect, a quantity surveyor and general contracting company for the design and construction of a new car-production plant. Continuous communication between all the project participants provides assurance that the evolving designed

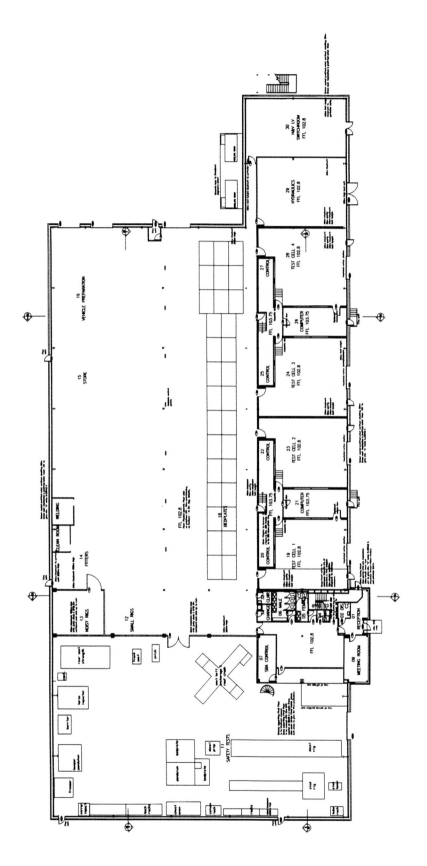

Fig. 5.5 CAD information exchange in client/architect design partnering for a new plant.

building form and materials are meeting the client's plant operating requirements simultaneously with the client's construction cost and time requirements. The same type of 3D CAD graphical information on the evolving building design can be transferred to and from the client's Computervision system and the architect's AutoCAD system to demonstrate the integration of building and manufacturing equipment as an evolving fully-integrated plant for car production.

Other types of client are experimenting with the systems used in the manufacturing industries to pre-design some of their new facilities in order to brief their architects more precisely. For example, the British Airports Authority, as a client briefing for new airport terminals with the ICAD system, previously mentioned as being used for automotive design. In this situation, the client can start to model, through their own experiential knowledge, the key dimensional design criteria for airport terminal, spatial sizes and arrangements (for example, the dimensional requirement 'rules' for locating the connection between the terminal satellites and the aircraft entrance and the baggage handling system). How the product modelling 'object' basis of these systems can be applied to building design through simpler and lower-cost applications is discussed further in Chapter 7.

Summary

■ The manufacturing industries are using CAD-related computer systems to benefit their own design and production processes. More advanced intelligent systems are being developed in practice.

■ As clients, their expectation will be that the construction industry will be using the self-same systems to improve communication in briefing and the design of their building plants and facilities.

CAD-related
and
other
systems
in
architecture
and
building

CAD applications for representing and presenting building form and material

As described in Chapter 2, advances in the research and development of available software for computer-aided design for architecture and building have been mainly in the field of computer-aided graphics. The software suppliers, aware of their markets, have been developing graphics systems that provide the user with both working and presentation capabilities that are attractive to architects and their clients and now almost impossible to resist! The majority of architects, who in the 1970s and 1980s generally resisted the computer as a potential design tool, would nowadays not see themselves as true professionals without having some sort of CAD graphics system as a major piece of their working equipment. Even the many one-man bands that make up quite a high proportion of the architectural profession would now not be without the 'Mac'. Most architects now use CAD graphics systems in their day-to-day work, essentially for the following two reasons:-

☐ to create a 3D representation and presentation image of their building form proposals; and

☐ to create a 2D representation and presentation images of the floor/ceiling/roof plans, internal cross-sections, internal/external elevations, and assembly details of the building elements that divide, support and enclose the building forms.

The degree of realism that can be created in the 3D presentations and the ease by which 3D views can be generated from 2D representations are largely a feature of the type and cost of the particular CAD software application one uses. However, realism in the representation and presentation of building form and material is good enough and vastly superior to previous paper-based presentations even with comparatively low-cost CAD systems. This is demonstrated in Figs 6.1–6.4 which show exterior and interior views of proposed building forms and material finishes.

The 3D presentations help architects to communicate the appearance of their conceptualization of a proposed building form and its material to their clients, planning authorities, engineers, construction managers and specialist trade contractors. If the 3D representation can then become animated, the building's 'appearance' as one moves around or through its enclosed form can also be communicated by the architect. Therefore the largest single benefit that current 3D CAD graphics applications are bringing towards achieving an agreed building solution in practice is in demonstrating the material finish and form of building elements. In other words all other project participants can see the same realistic appearance that the architect sees and agree upon it or not!

Fig. 6.1 CAD external view.

Fig. 6.2 CAD interior view.

It is also possible using some very sophisticated 3D CAD graphics animation to demonstrate how the building form proposed by the architect could cope with the 'shape' requirements of a client's particular activity. For example, how a piece of equipment could pass between or through building elements. In addition, 3D graphics modelling systems can also be used to analyse engineering technical performance functions of a particular building element component assembly. This is demonstrated as a sequence from a 'walk thru' application in Fig. 6.5.

With the addition of some dimensional data this animation could be extended to demonstrate the size and shape of some aspect of people movement that would be a concern of the client's design for the building as a managed facility.

So then, CAD 3D graphics representations and presentations are essentially helping to transfer 'appearance' information within an ideal integrated design process as described in Chapter 4. They can also help in a limited way to transfer 'activity

Fig. 6.3 CAD external view.

requirement' and some 'technical performance' information between architects, engineers and specialist trade contractor designers, with the potential for additional spatial features in the future.

CAD applications for representing and presenting building structure and environment

CAD graphics systems, when based on 3D modelling, also provide the means by which the structural and environmental implications of the proposed building's form and material can be calculated. Taking the files of the graphics system's model, calculations can be made directly from the generated spatial geometry for heating and ventilation loads based on pre-defined heat loss values of external envelopes. CAD-related systems can then, even now, be used to generate for example the detail design and assembled component parts of a mechanical ventilation system.

This is demonstrated in Fig. 6.6 which shows a specialist engineering system generated from the CAD-system files of a particular building form and material.

Similarly, the files of the generated element geometry of a structural frame form and material can be directly used by a structural calculating package to either check or create a proposed structural system in terms of sizes and arrangement of assembled structural elements for pre-defined live and dead load values. This is demonstrated in Fig. 6.7 which shows a specialist structural engineering system generated from the CAD-system files of a particular building element form.

With the addition of some specialist contractor component resources data further related to the generated files, the actual production time and cost could also be predicted, directly from the original proposed building spatial and elemental form and material.

Fig. 6.4 CAD interior view.

Fig. 6.5 CAD interior space animation sequence.

So then, CAD 3D graphics representation and presentation are also helping to transfer performance information within theideal integrated design process described in Chapter 4. They can also help, with the addition of non-graphical alpha-numeric data, to transfer technical performance and production information between architects, engineers and specialist trade contractors.

CAD applications for representing and presenting building element and component assembly resources

CAD 2D – and to a limited extent 3D – graphics representations and presentations are by and large being used by architects to computerize their traditional scheme and detail design drawings. For the architect, the differences in terms of drawing production from the manual methods are that:

☐ graphical symbols of components and elements can be created, stored and rapidly accessed to create and change the 2D views of building spaces and their dividing and enclosing elements; and

☐ the graphical symbols can be pre-defined so that they can be automatically measured for linear, area and volumetric quantities and discreet component location and scheduling.

The immediate benefit over former paper-based methods comes in the actual production of the information in terms of the drawing and measuring of the proposed building elements and components. The activity of both can be carried out simultaneously by the architect. This could represent a saving in time and

Fig. 6.6 CAD-related environmental design.

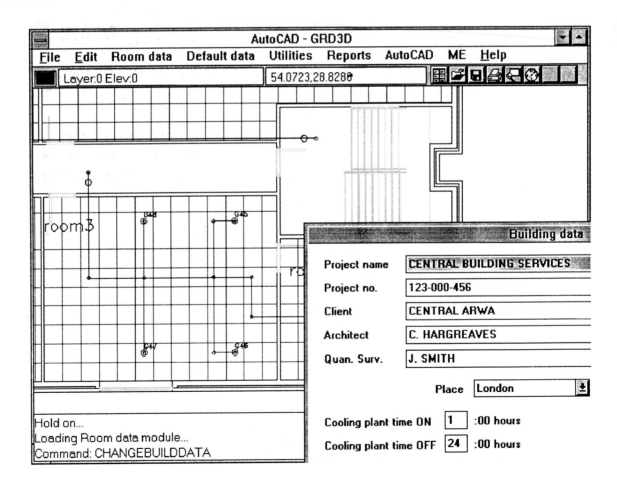

cost of a separate quantity surveying activity and part engineering measurement activity. It also means that when the drawn building design proposals are changed as a result of design development, the related measurements are automatically changed for up-dated quantities and calculations. Current CAD-related systems that now have integral databases will also allow for the creation of measurement rules for more precise measurement of component sizes. This is demonstrated Figs 6.8 and 6.9 which show a particular building component or material measurement direct from CAD 2D and 3D graphics files.

With the addition of other rules, for at the very least costings but possibly time and sequence for constructing these elements, a direct relationship with the overall construction management for

Fig. 6.7 CAD-related structural design.

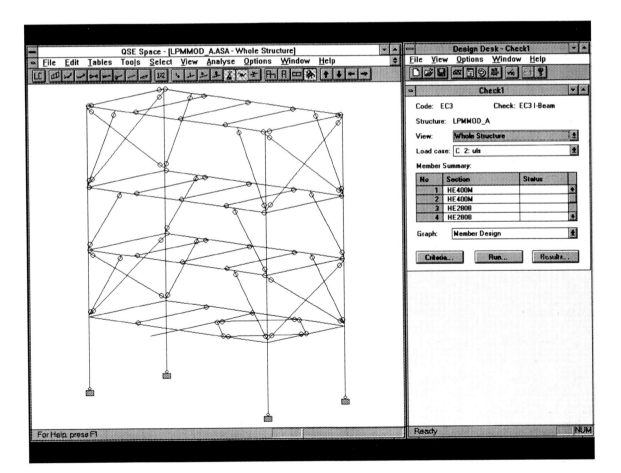

the building's production can be achieved from these CAD-generated files.

Although programme management computer-based systems can provide information on resource time, loading and sequence already exist, they are not yet CAD-related.

So then, CAD 2D and 3D graphics representations and presentations are essentially helping to transfer production information within the ideal integrated design process described in Chapter 4. When directly linked with the particular element performance calculating systems, they can also help transfer technical performance and production information between architects and specialist trade contractors.

Fig. 6.8 CAD-related resource quantities from a 3D representation.

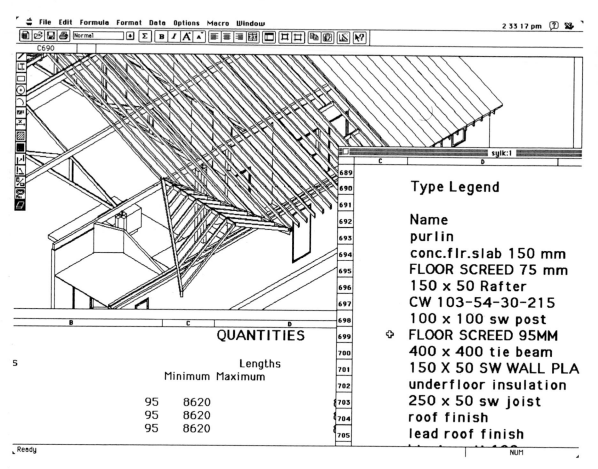

CAD applications for representing and presenting buildings – current and potential use

Overall, current 2D and 3D CAD graphics representations and presentations and related alpha-numeric data are able to transfer material content information between the architect and the engineer for calculating technical performances of specific elements. Similarly, such information passes between the architect and the specialist contractor for calculating technical engineering performance and measuring the material quantity content for technical production of specific elements. In theory, and with an integrated management approach to building projects, they are capable of supporting an integrated design which could occur simultaneously between all the project participants.

Fig. 6.9 CAD-related resource quantities from a 2D representation.

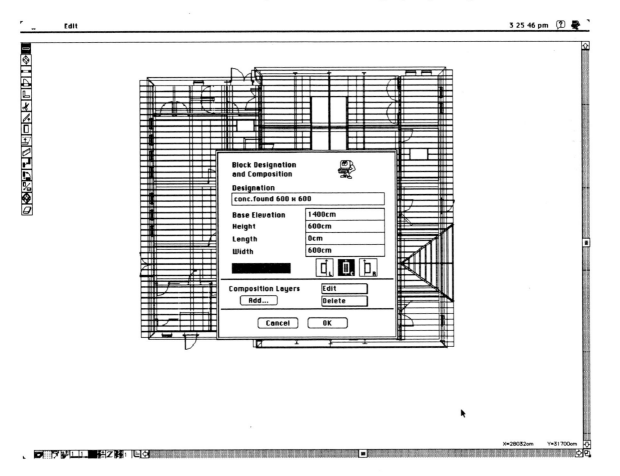

The CAD-related system applications currently available are being used in different ways in the different phases of a building project. Although these phases are still being carried out sequentially, they could be carried out simultaneously by using the CAD-related systems in a more integrated manner. This would only be possible, however, following changes in building project working practices which allowed each project participant to work in partnership, the partnership being both contractual (as discussed in Chapter 3), and in a co-designing sense (as proposed in Chapter 4). Even then there are still some gaps in available CAD-related and other systems in practice.

Table 6.1 shows what is, and is not, currently available in order to support a fully-integrated design process. The table brings together the ways in which a building project passes through phases, the fact that one project participant takes the essential design lead in that phase and the IT tools that could support their design contribution. The columns of the table are indicated as:

☐ the project phase;
☐ the project participant(s) primarily involved in the particular phase; and
☐ the type of computer-based information processing method that can currently encapsulate the prime participants' knowledge for transmission to another participant dealing with another phase.

It is interesting to note that all the above programmes that deal with the quantification of either material, time or money are based on standard computer database and spreadsheet system applications. Even proprietory software systems, such as project-management and facility management packages, have these generic applications as their basis. In some instances, it is even being discovered in practice that slight customization of the basic standard database and spreadsheet packages for resource time and cost control might be more useful than the proprietry packages.

Table 6.1 Software systems currently available

Phase	Participants	Information processing methods
Briefing	Client	None*
Design	Architect	Fabric element calculating and detail design programmes
	Engineer	Structural and services element calculating and detail design programmes
Specifying	Architect/engineer	Standard materials and workmanship clause programmes
		Bills of materials
	Quantity surveyor	Bills of quantities (UK-specific practice)
	Specialist trade contractor	Specialist element detail design programmes
Tendering	Construction manager	Schedules of rates programmes
		Bills of materials programmes
	Specialist trade contractor	Schedule of rates programmes
		Bills of materials programmes
Construction	Construction manager	Construction time and sequence programmes
		Materials scheduling, ordering and delivery programmes
		Element stage invoicing programmes
	Specialist trade contractor	Specialist element delivery, installation and invoicing programmes
Managing and maintaining	Client	Element maintenance (facility management) programmes

*Although any particular client may have computer-based systems to support their business, they would appear to have none that adequately describe their business operations and activities in order for them to directly translate into briefing for a building.

Other non-CAD-related systems that support the work processes of all project participants

The CAD-related systems described above are either algorithmic calculating systems, databases, spreadsheets or, in some instances, rule-based parametric macros as part of the CAD application itself. The latter is close to the expert systems in the field of artificial intelligence, but is inflexible in terms of the addition of any new knowledge by the user. The database/spreadsheet applications can be an integral part of the CAD system in some instances, but in others is a separate system to which the CAD graphics files can be exported.

However, these generic database/spreadsheet applications, as well as other programming, document control and word-processing applications, are also being used by each project participant for their own internal project and business management processes. Some of the applications currently being developed for architectural and engineering practices and construction companies will provide the potential to manage information on:

☐ potential client contacts for marketing purposes;
☐ past project histories for feedback purposes;
☐ staff cvs for skills, knowledge and project-type experience;

which all support the winning of new business for the firm;

☐ staff skill time requirements and records;
☐ staff costs related to time and staged income;
☐ task definition, time and sequence;

which all support the efficient and economic running of an individual project by the firm;

☐ technical data on buildings for design guidance;
☐ quality, environmental and health/safety procedures; and
☐ company financial accounting, salaries and invoicing;

which all support the efficient and economic running of the organization as a business.

Examples of some of these applications are shown in Figs 6.10 and 6.11.

Although these applications are not directly used in the knowledge sharing and information exchange between the separate project participants in the design of a building, they are being

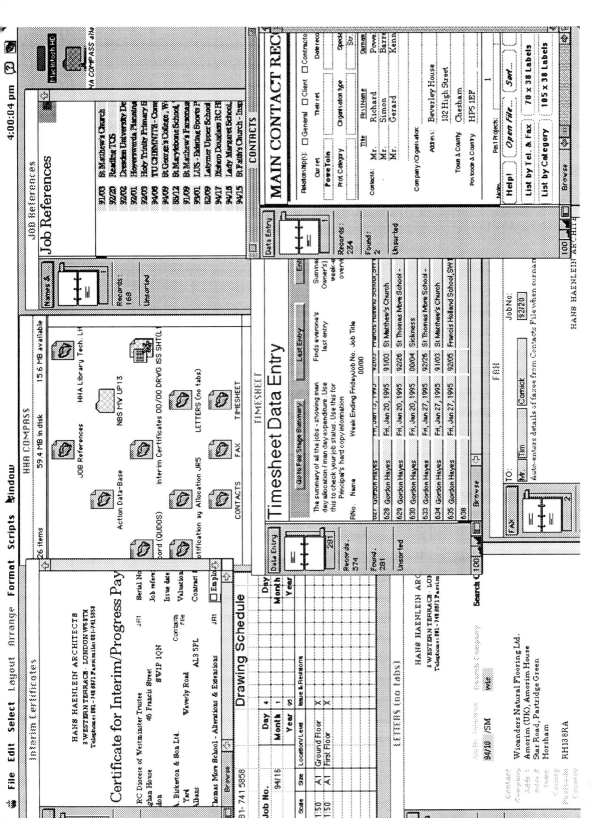

Fig. 6.10 Computer-based architectural practice administration support system.

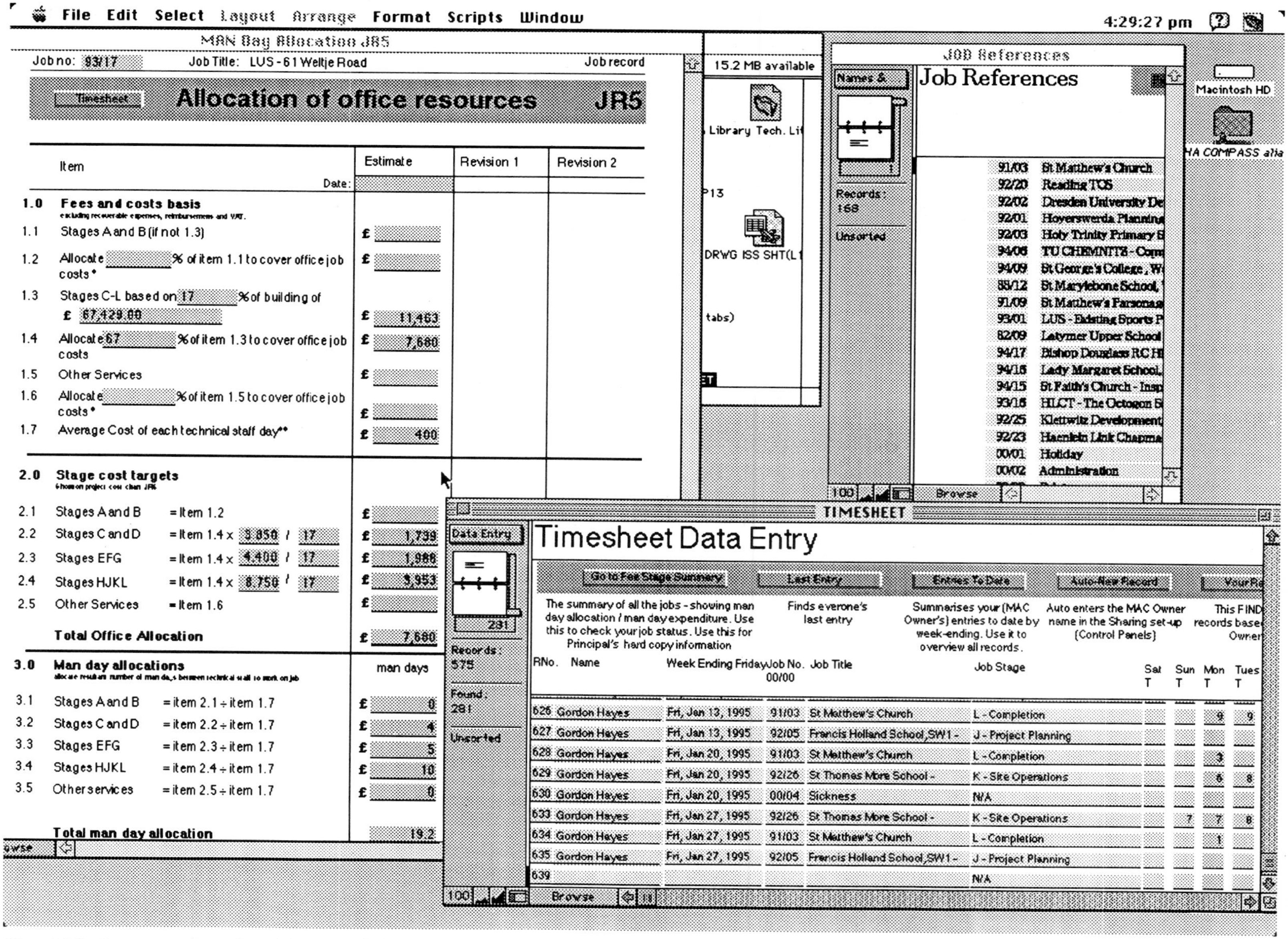

Fig. 6.11 Computer-based architect's job book.

used for knowledge sharing and information exchange within each project participant's own organization.

Given that the actual generic computer-based applications being used are the same as those that are CAD-related in the design of the building, they could also provide an integrated information link between the project and the business of each participant. For example, in actually producing the CAD-drawn design, the design organization could be automatically logging the time they are spending as a business on any particular project.

In effect, these applications can provide the downward information integration within the separate businesses involved in the building project, whereas the formerly described CAD-related applications provide information integration across these businesses during the course of the project. These would then support the link between project management at the higher level with that at the lower level described in Chapter 3 and shown in Fig. 3.2.

Summary

- Current CAD systems have been developed and are used to improve visualization of the appearance of a proposed building design.
- 3D animation and photorealism techniques further improve appearance visualization by simulating human movement around and within the proposed building design.
- CAD-related database, spreadsheet, calculating and rule-based parametric applications can now deal with all other non-visual aspects of a proposed building design.
- CAD-related applications can be used for both information integration between project participants and within project participants to link project and business management.

Computer
integrated
construction –
techniques
and
tools

Objectives for integrating tools

The changes required in project management and approaches to design methods in order to achieve integration are described in Chapters 3 and 4. Current CAD applications in architecture, building and other industries that are moving towards integration are described in Chapters 5 and 6. A fundamental conceptual model for integration was proposed in Chapter 2. The purpose of this chapter is to describe the emerging computer-based tools and computer-related techniques that will ultimately make building design integration possible in practice.

A review of the requirements for building design integration from previous chapters tells us that computer tools and techniques must be able to:

☐ allow for the exchange of information between one computer system and another;
☐ process and present diverse information concerning building appearance, performance, cost and time simultaneously;
☐ present information in the most appropriate format for the project participant who needs to react to it as part of the project process; and
☐ permit different project participants (who may be in different locations) to share computer data.

Information should be both the raw geometric and non-geometric data and its meaning and exchange should be possible between different generic types and makes of computer system. The different generic types of computer systems are:

☐ 2D, 3D and animation CAD graphics systems
☐ performance calculating systems

□ production activity time and sequence calculating systems
□ component, material and labour quantity and cost calculating systems
□ rule-based parametric design systems and
□ descriptive textual systems

The ability to exchange data between different makes of system will permit marketplace freedom for any participating company or practice to own their own system, which they can use from project to project. Information integration should also be possible between project information and company or practice business information, for example, the automatic recording of time spent/money earned by a designer or building operative as they make their day-to-day contribution to the project.

The objectives for computer-based integrating tools and techniques should be that at reasonable cost and convenience they should be able to support:

□ the exploration of an increased number of project solution alternatives
□ multi-criteria evaluation of any design solution at any stage in the project process
□ a particular project participant's specific explanation of a problem and its proposed solution
□ reduction in time of each participant's input and
□ the maintenance of information integrity when it is passed on to a more detailed design activity in subsequent project phases.

For the purposes of further explanation in this chapter, the tools are the software systems currently available that can in any way contribute to information integration, and the techniques are the underlying principles and application of those tools.

Tools available for integration

Computer systems are continually being developed by the software and hardware vendors to improve their own market position. Each stage of this development makes the application of the systems more user-friendly and, most significantly for building design, makes ever more convenient the ability to transfer information immediately from one form of data to another (for example graphics to text). The tools currently available and the way in which they support building design geometry information integration are shown in Fig. 7.1.

These 2D/3D CAD systems generate spatial and element geometry files of a proposed building form, which can be directly and

Fig. 7.1 CAD-generated 3D building geometry – visual arrangement of structural form and interior.

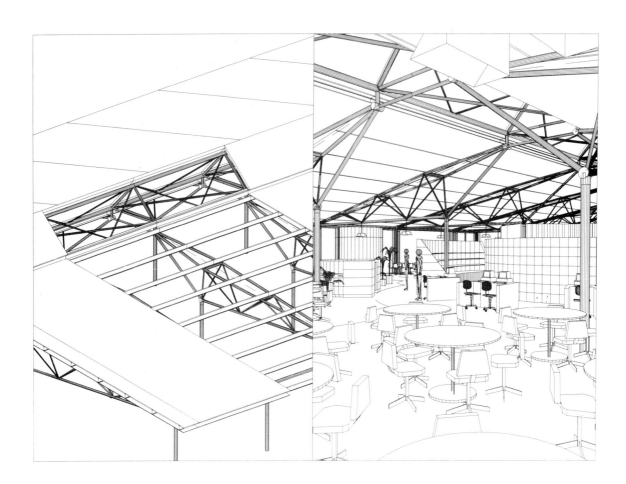

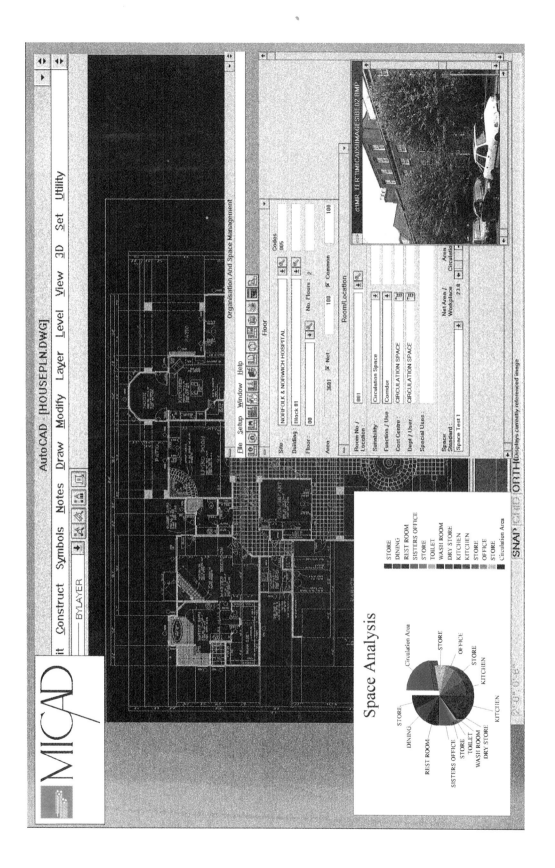

Fig. 7.2 Cost-related capital and facility operating resources.

immediately read and understood by the systems for the purposes shown in Figs 7.2–7.5.

Figure 7.2 shows a spreadsheet system generating cost-related component, material quantity and specification values in order to simultaneously evaluate whether the client's capital construction and facility-running cost requirements are being met.

Figure 7.3 shows a programming system generating time-related element assembly or installation activity duration and sequence values in order to simultaneously evaluate meeting the client's time requirements.

Figure 7.4 shows a system for generating structure-related performance values in order to simultaneously evaluate, through a structural calculating system, whether structural stability requirements were being met. Equally feasibly, this may be a calculating system generating energy-related performance values

Fig. 7.3 Time-related element assembly duration and sequence.

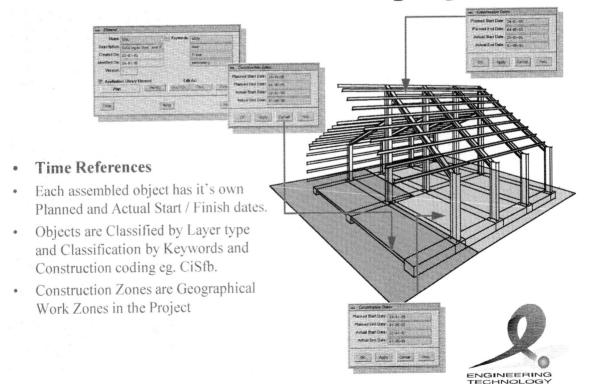

Element Time Stamping

- **Time References**
- Each assembled object has it's own Planned and Actual Start / Finish dates.
- Objects are Classified by Layer type and Classification by Keywords and Construction coding eg. CiSfb.
- Construction Zones are Geographical Work Zones in the Project

ENGINEERING
TECHNOLOGY

in order to simultaneously evaluate whether the client's energy use costs targets are met.

Figure 7.5 shows a rule-based system generating either fabric, structure or services element assembly code complying solutions automatically from the values generated by the systems shown in Figs 7.2–7.4. The generic types of computer system application above can support the exchange and integrated processing of the basic diverse types of information generated during the course of a building project. The fact that all the information about the final building solution has been generated and integrated using these computer systems means that it can now also be comprehensively stored. This in turn provides an integrated information model of the final building itself and its performance values.

Fig. 7.4 Energy-related and structure-related building operating performance.

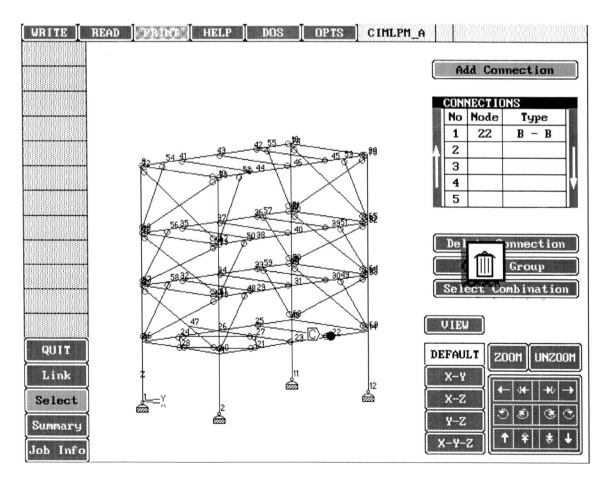

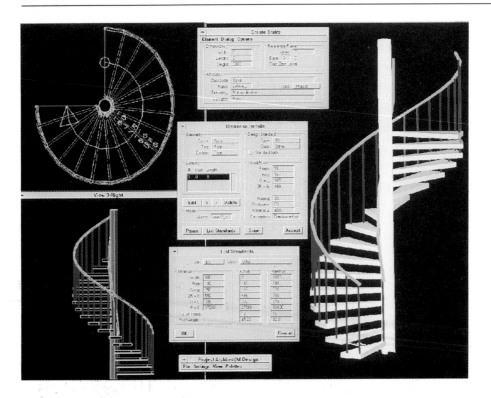

Fig. 7.5 Rule-related element performance compliance.

However, with the addition of computer system applications that deal with document and decision control, further information could be integrated that describes the decision-making process of the project. The new document management system applications which are becoming available provide such a tool for this purpose. As the information represented in any document (for example a design drawing) is usually based on other information in another document (for example a design code), document management can provide a basis for design decision tracing. The usefulness of this capability is two-fold. In the first instance, it will provide the document control, design control and design change control for ISO 9000 quality assurance management during the project. Secondly, it will provide a useful project history for feedback after the project is completed.

In other words, by using all these integrated system applications the information model will comprise both the product as well as the process of the building project. This will be of value to architects, engineers and construction managers for their own professional project management development, as well as to clients for their on-going facility management of the completed building.

Finally by integrating all the above project management information with their business management information, each project participant will have more control over resource contribution during the project as well as being able to refer back to it for future projects. This will then support their actual business.

What will enable these tools to be used in practice with increasing ease and effectiveness are the following current and emerging techniques that underpin their development and use.

Figures 7.6 and 7.7 show typical outputs from the type of system now available that can process and present the type of information previously described.

Fig. 7.6 Project quality management procedure-related control.

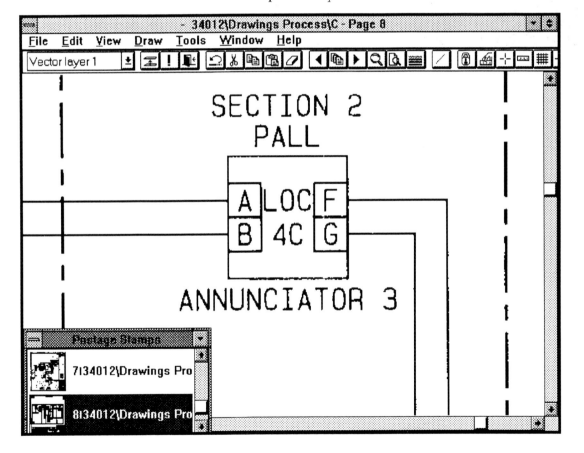

Current and emerging techniques for integration

Computer development, in both the construction and manufacturing fields of application, has been moving towards the support for integration. This has been due to an implicit demand by those industries for the future integration of their design, production and maintenance processes, in order to improve business practice. In addition, information integration is obviously possible because of the nature of computer system applications themselves – computers can deal with increasingly large amounts of diverse types of information, as well as providing relationships between different types of information from different generating sources.

In building projects, as well as product manufacturing, a fundamental and historic method used in the design process has

Fig. 7.7 Business quality management procedure-related control.

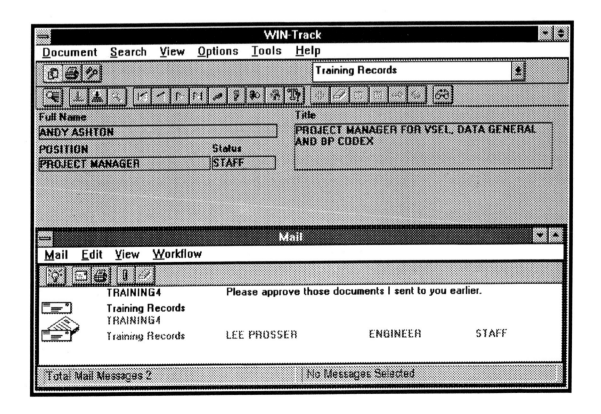

been the generation of drawings that visualize the physical geometry of the building or product to be constructed or manufactured. Drawings used commonly understood graphical symbols to represent the shapes of the component parts of the building or product and how they were to be assembled. They were also used to represent the overall appearance of the finished building or product. Computer applications began by computerizing these representational graphical symbols. CAD in its basic form was, and in fact still is, only computer-aided drawing rather than computer-aided design. Drawings, whether produced manually or by computer, are only useful in the design process because the people generating them and reading them understand what the symbols mean through experiential knowledge. Of themselves drawings are information poor, but are none the less a powerful visual means to which information can be applied and from which it can be extracted because of the knowledge of the person generating or reading the drawing.

The key to being able to design with the CAD systems lies in the fact that the digitized drawing is a visualizing 'front end', through the drawing's supporting files, to diverse sorts of data. And it is this data which contains the diverse types of information which can be used to create and understand the design. In effect, the computerized drawing represents diverse types of information about the drawn objects in an already implied way. The activity of designing through CAD is therefore supported because the computer can automatically manipulate and relate the information which is represented by drawn objects and their arrangements. What is actually drawn is the geometry of the object – what is actually used in the process of design is the knowledge applied to the information about the object's attributes.

The key to integrated design is the ability of each participant 'designer' to be able to reason with their own knowledge simultaneously with the other participants' using relevant attribute information generated by the drawn object's geometry. This relationship between an object's drawn geometry, its attribute information and the participants' 'designer's reasoning' is best illustrated by taking the example of a structural column in a

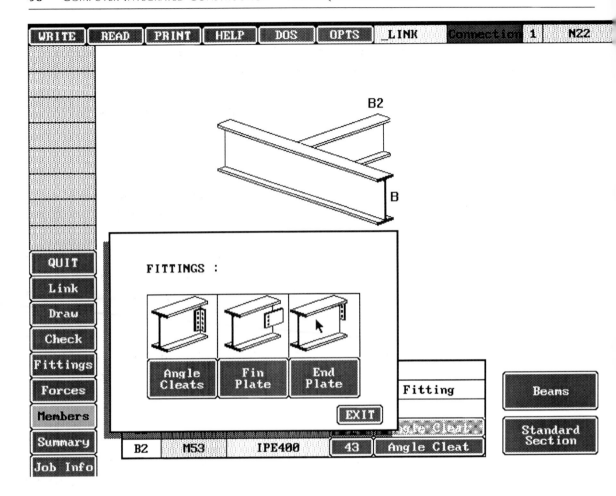

Fig. 7.8 A CAD-generated building element 'object', attribute and design reasoning.

building (Fig. 7.8). In this example, the common drawn object of a beam-to-beam junction has different conceptual and physical attributes, each of which are relevant to the reasoning of a particular project participant 'designer'. Given a particular size, shape and material content:

☐ To the client, the object represents a physical element in enclosed space, or part of an exterior, that may or may not support the desired appearance and/or efficient operations to be carried out and will need to be maintained once the building is in use as a facility.

☐ To the architect, the object represents an architectural feature that, through its shape and location, will have a perceived visual and functional impact on the overall architectural spatial enclosure and/or exterior.

☐ To the structural engineer, the object represents a structural element that will transmit forces and perform as part of an overall structural system to support the loads to be carried by the enclosed space.

☐ To the service engineer, the object represents a physical element that may or may not support the installation of all or any of the services needed to control the environment of the enclosed space.

☐ To the specialist trade contractor, the object represents a construction element to be designed in detail and realized by off- and/or on-site production through the application of skilled work, material and plant.

☐ To the construction manager, the object represents a construction element that may or may not support the overall management of the construction of the enclosed space by others to meet a given construction cost and time target.

If the final size, shape, location and material content of the object is to be an integrated design decision, then the computer system must be able to send and return digitized information in a format that can be recognized by all of the systems described in Figs 7.1–7.5. The computer techniques that will allow this to happen now, and certainly in the immediate future, are described in the following sections.

The current layering conventions

All CAD systems are based on the fact that each symbol or set of symbols that are drawn are classified by the user, first by code, into classes or layers. This means that particular drawn object sets, for example the structural frame, have supporting files to which other non-graphical alpha-numeric data can be directly related. It is therefore the files that are exchanged between system and system and not the drawings. Even though the drawings themselves can be exchanged as ultimate input and ultimate output between systems, it is in fact the files that are being exchanged.

Current CAD systems can even pass classified and layered files to a variety of other systems for the processing of drawn sets of discrete objects. The most obvious, and possibly most effective, being where the 'object files' of the drawn element's geometry (for example a concrete structural frame) can be passed to a database/spreadsheet system for automatic material and cost calculation based on given rates from a specialist trade contractor. This is because, by and large and when the material content is specified, the constructed element's cost has a direct relationship to the designed element's geometry, that is to say its size, shape and arrangement.

Other systems which deal with knowledge that is essentially geometric-specific (that is to say which use dimensional rules related to the length, height, area or volume of an element object) are also capable of having a direct and appropriate data relationship to the CAD graphics systems. An example would be those that can calculate the amount of air exchange that an enclosed space requires and that can then generate the detail design of an appropriate ventilation system. Figure 7.9 shows a typical output from the type of system now available.

However, there are two sorts of limitation to achieving comprehensive information integration with just the current layering conventions alone. The first is that no direct information exchange can be made between the CAD graphics and other systems dealing with other project participants' 'designer's knowledge' that is not just geometric specific (for example, where the knowledge concerns information that is about a particular work sequence of a specific specialist trade contractor's construction of a structural element). The second limitation, and one which is far more serious in terms of simultaneous designing, is described in the following situation.

An architect creates the architectural geometric model of a whole building using a 2D/3D CAD graphics system. Through the layering convention, the relevant geometric information is passed to a services engineer's H&V system which automatically calculates loads for, say, space ventilation, and a system to provide them. However, should those loads be unacceptable in terms of the client's energy cost targets, but would become acceptable if the geometric model was amended, such an amended model could not be automatically passed back to the original model in the architect's CAD graphics system.

In other words, information exchange between the architect and services engineer using the most recent and commonly available CAD graphics systems, is still only one way, the spatial geometric model always having to be generated first. This is true even when the other system has to deal only with geometric-specific information, for example in the case of material quantity

Fig. 7.9 A CAD-generated building space, calculated ventilation requirement and ventilation system assembly.

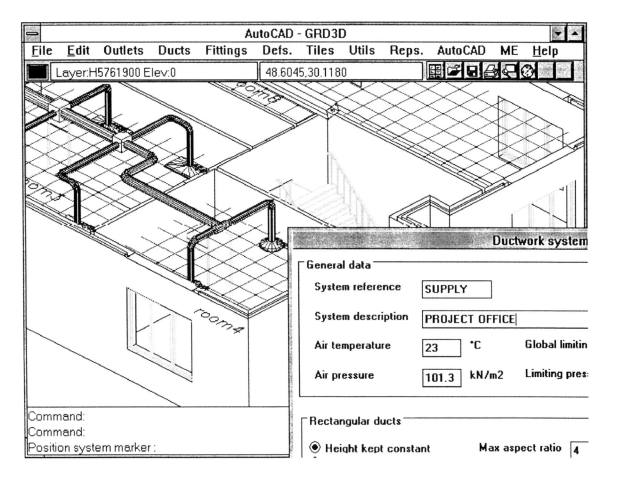

cost. To overcome both these limitations other techniques have to be applied to computer systems.

The emerging object-oriented approach

As described in Chapter 1, a great amount of basic and applied research has been, and is still being, carried out into how diverse and non-graphical information can be directly exchanged in building projects using the computer. Employing computer languages and techniques that were first applied in the field of artificial intelligence, a general approach has been developed in which:

☐ objects have attributes, one of which is their geometry which can be viewed by a CAD graphics system;
☐ databases contain the non-geometric attribute descriptions of objects using 'natural' computer languages; and
☐ data-structures follow agreed standards and information, that is to say alpha-numeric data with semantic meaning, and can be exchanged between systems.

What happens as a result of this approach is again best described by using an experimental situation.

We have four linked computer systems in which the first describes the geometry of the architectural form, the second decribes the geometry of the structural frame (these first two are therefore CAD graphics systems), the third describes the structural calculations of the frame and the fourth the work sequence time and duration of construction operations (these last two are therefore non-graphical calculating systems). Using the above approach, when the architectural form is changed, the other three system descriptions (both graphical and non-graphical) automatically change to suit the new form.

What is important about this approach, in which the computer systems recognize the graphically-represented objects as described real objects with attributes rather than just lines on paper, is that meaningful information has now been exchanged, in much the same way as would happen intellectually between human experts. In other words, simultaneous designing for spatial form, structural system and construction operational planning can now occur. However, because all knowledge-based reasoning, and the information it requires and produces, has to be related to a spatial geometric form, even with this advanced method the essential information will always be generated first by the architect's CAD graphics system. This situation is true in the application of human knowledge using non-computer manual methods, and will also be true using computer methods. All knowledge of the other project participants can only be applied and related once the geometry of a building object has first been defined.

Object-oriented databases using AI techniques are already incorporated in some bespoke and customized systems for particular organizations. For example, a major European construction company producing housing has a system that will automatically change construction cost and time when the geometric form of the housing plans are changed. The development of international STEP standards for data structures will, in the not so distant future, enable a much greater ease and accessability of information exchange between system and system, whether those systems are essentially graphical or alpha-numerical, regardless of the software vendor. The current layering conventions of all 2D/3D CAD graphics systems provide the fundamental basis upon which these future developments can take place and become readily and widely available to the construction industry. This is because the layers can become entities and the entities can become objects. This then means that third party software systems (for example those that can calculate any time or cost of performance aspect of either the building product or process) can be written for direct application to a CAD graphics system. Analysis calculations of any of these aspects can then be made direct from the CAD graphical files either working within the CAD system itself or outside the CAD system using transferred files.

The following example from a major EU ESPRIT research project shows the file exchange between one CAD system and another. However, this information exchange is not just the transfer of the graphical symbols from one digitized drawing to another. The files from the first CAD system have been exported to an object-oriented database and the second CAD system has read them. In essence, this means that it is not just the drawing that has been exchanged but the meaning of the drawing, that is to say real objects with their attributes. It is this ability to, in effect, exchange the attribute information of the drawn building objects that will form the essential basis of computer-integrated building design.

Figure 7.10 shows a typical output from the type of system now available that can process and present this type of information.

Windows, networking and EDI

The most recent developments in reasonably low-cost PC-based computing are also making integration between the various designers that all contribute to a building project that much more realizable. These developments are those that are helping to create a working environment using computers which support interactive working by different users over space and time with different systems.

The new Windows technology and the working environment that it creates now available with all PC-based systems allows system users to:

☐ work in a common way in terms of information storage, retrieval and processing regardless of which software system is being used;

☐ work on and view multiple documents simultaneously using different types of computer systems such as CAD graphics, database, spreadsheet, calculating systems and word-processing software; and

☐ make immediate transfer of files dealing with alpha-numeric text (and possibly even those that support object geometry graphics) from one document to another.

This technique will therefore support the simultaneous viewing of different types of information being used by different project participant designers. This in itself starts to provide an improved information environment in which integrated designing can occur. Figure 7.11 shows a typical output from the type of system currently available.

Fig. 7.10 CAD-generated geometry – system to system.

When the technique of networking is added to that of Windows, there is an even more useful support for integrated

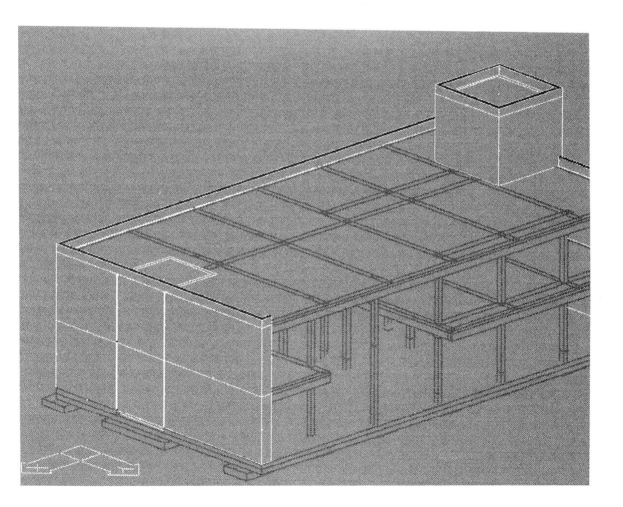

designing during a building project. It will further allow system users to:

☐ work at different locations simultaneously and
☐ work on the same graphical or non-graphical information in, what is in effect, shared data space in the computer.

Fig. 7.11 CAD-generated building geometry, material quantities, work programme and space performance-in-use in a Windows environment.

This technique will therefore support separate location working by different project participant designers, working from say different divisions in the same organization or, most likely in the majority of building projects, different organizations.

Finally, the ability to communicate over long distances through dedicated, or even normal, telephone lines through Email and

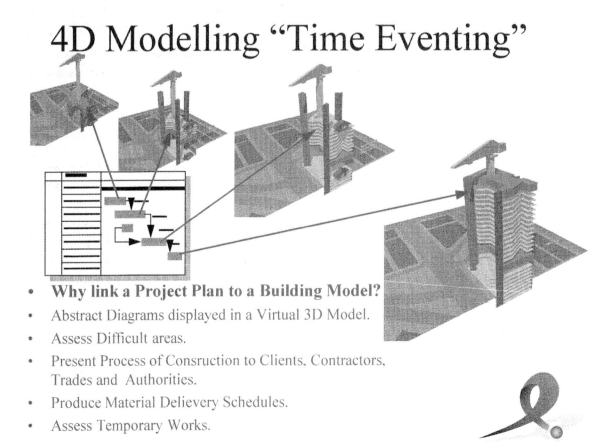

4D Modelling "Time Eventing"

- **Why link a Project Plan to a Building Model?**
- Abstract Diagrams displayed in a Virtual 3D Model.
- Assess Difficult areas.
- Present Process of Consruction to Clients, Contractors, Trades and Authorities.
- Produce Material Delievery Schedules.
- Assess Temporary Works.

ENGINEERING
TECHNOLOGY

Electronic Data Interchange means that all project participant designers can work together even from remote locations. With new computer-based systems that will deal with the management aspects of building projects, such as document control and quality assurance audit, improved and more systematic control, tracking and archiving of integrated design information will be both encouraged and supported. Therefore, the way in which these designers can work together to come to a common solution can be controlled better as a process and recorded for review and feedback once the design activity is completed.

These particular techniques, which are affecting the way in which all business activity is carried out in which information has to be transferred and processed, will be used, and expected to be used, in building projects. Many official reports have already been produced detailing these ideas and the potential benefits. As suggested in Chapter 5, the expectation of certainly industrial and commercial clients that these techniques *will* be used will be because they are using them to support their own business processes.

Summary

- The emerging tools and techniques to support integrated design for building are becoming available through existing software systems.
- The tools will allow the transfer of information between systems in a way that will support shared knowledge between designers.
- The techniques will support a shared computer-based working environment in which each designer will be able to exchange information with meaning through computer-based systems.
- These tools and techniques will be increasingly used by the construction industry's clients who in turn will expect them to be used in the building design process.

A
simulated
integrated
project
using
computer
tools
and
techniques

Objectives of the simulation

In the previous chapters the project management methods and current and emerging tools and techniques that support integrated building design have been described. In the opening chapters a conceptual model, based on previous building project management applied research was proposed as being fundamental to these integrating applications in practice. Given that not all the necessary tools and techniques are widely and freely available in practice, especially to small to medium-sized practices, the demonstration in this simulation will be limited. However, even a consideration of the limitations will be a benefit in that it will reveal the existence of gaps in either the computer tools and techniques or the project being managed.

The objectives of the simulation are to take a small to medium-sized live building project where a computer-based system is currently being applied and to demonstrate the following aspects of integrated design as may be applied in building design and construction management practice in the near future:

☐ How the client's building use requirements, construction cost and time requirements, and site constraining feature requirements are being defined in terms of acceptance criteria to be satisfied by a scheme design proposal.
☐ How the architect's scheme design proposal(s) are shown, both graphically and in alpha-numeric text, in order to meet these acceptance criteria.
☐ How the agreed scheme design will be carried forward in various aspects of an engineer's structure, fabric and services detail in order to maintain the satisfaction of these acceptance criteria.

☐ How the agreed scheme and detail design will be carried forward in various aspects of a construction manager's production design for the whole building and how various aspects of a specialist trade contractor's production design for a particular element will maintain the satisfaction of these acceptance criteria.

☐ How the production designs are carried forward to whole building and specific element construction control to maintain acceptance criteria satisfaction and how all design and construction information is finally archived for the client's facility management plan so that the satisfaction of the acceptance criteria is maintained.

The simulation will therefore demonstrate how the people in the participating organizations will be able to manage their own work in terms of information input and output using computer-based systems. It will therefore show the necessary operating procedures that need to be carried out by each and every project participant, as a designer, and how the computer-based systems are being used to exchange information at the critical points in the overall process.

The project process with information input and output

The building process is one in which the project first conceived by the client passes through a series of sequential phases in which information is both the input from the preceding phase and output to a subsequent one. At each iteration of preceding, current and subsequent phases the information that exists is added to in value by further information that is provided by a particular project participant's expert knowledge. The phases of the project in which designing is occurring must, by definition, be those that occur, and are preferably completed, before the constructing phase begins. In each phase, each project participant as designer will contribute from their knowledge according to the degree to which their knowledge is required.

The terms used in Chapter 2 to describe each phase are those proposed by the author and others for a 'quality management model for building projects'. The terms reflect the traditional view of the process of a project and therefore designing is the term used for the phase in which the traditional designers, that is the architects and engineers, contribute the most from their knowledge. What are important, however, are the described objectives of each phase, as they will dictate the essential designing purpose of that particular phase. Finally, the reason for using the term phases instead of stages is to establish the idea that although there is an implied order to the sets of tasks needed to meet the objectives of each phase, the cycle of iteration could be so tight that the phases could in fact be simultaneous. What is important is that each phase represents a distinct objective which requires specific information input and output for the sets of tasks to realize the objective. The simple picture of the project phase objectives of the participant designers who contribute from their knowledge to each phase, and the information input, information added value and information output from each phase to another are shown on pp. 115 and 116. The way in which CAD-related tools and techniques are applied to the information input and output during the process is shown on pp. 117 and 118.

The final output of this process with computer applications should be two-fold. The first output is the integrated design which, through using the computer tools and techniques, will be in the form of an integrated information model. When the integrated design has been physically realized through the subsequent constructing phase, the second output will be the building itself. The integrated information model then becomes the basis upon which the building as a facility can be managed throughout the final maintaining/managing phase of the project process. Pages 119–139 show a combination of computer graphics or textual output images using an AutoCAD package related to simple databases, spreadsheets and word-processing along with a work process flow diagram to which each image is related. Where AutoCAD files could have been exported to other third-party software (for example HVAC calculating and design packages) the availability of this type of information exchange will be noted on the work process flow, if not actually imaged. It should also be assumed that the actual work flow process itself can ultimately become a computer output image, concurrently represented and displayed in a Windows environment. This means that, in principle, both the building design and the design process can be known simultaneously and archived for future reference.

The simulated project with computer applications

The actual live project in question is a leisure barn for a school that provides residential education and care for children with special needs. The client is an educational trust which sees the need for the barn as an important additional facility to the existing residential, leisure and education accommodation provision on the site. The outline of the building form has been agreed with the local planning authority and its spatial arrangement and location suits the existing built and natural environment of the site. The project is to be procured by the client using construction management with external specialist trade contractors and an internal workforce carrying various element packages of detail design and construction work. Essential user requirements of the barn are for relaxation of children and staff and simple games. Due to the children's special needs, the barn's interior fittings and finishes will need to be extremely robust and the internal appearance will need to be of low distraction. The link with the main building is to provide access to both the barn and media/computer/speech therapy accommodation. Within the barn an artroom with a play activity area above is to be accommodated. The remainder of the barn is to be space that can be varied in its furniture and fittings to accommodate a range of activities including:

☐ letting off steam by the children
☐ simple play activities between staff and children, e.g. basketball, parachute etc.

☐ creating interesting environments by children or by staff for children

☐ climbing up and over frames and ropes by children

☐ putting on shows by staff and children for parents and friends of the school

☐ running staff training courses in a range of working techniques

☐ inside space provision to supplement 'outside' summer garden party events

☐ staff and children individually exercising with equipment and

☐ music and dance activities by staff and children.

The barn will obviously have to meet all the general legislative and good practice design and construction management requirements related to a building and project of this type. It should also be accepted that during the briefing phase of this project a good personal rapport and understanding has been established between the client's project manager or representative, the architect and engineer, the construction manager and a key specialist trade contractor who will design and construct a steel frame and cladding system. The use of the computer tools and techniques was agreed as a necessary part of the process in that first phase so that each participant could work in a manner that allowed the direct exchange of information.

The following computer drawings and alpha-numeric software system outputs and work process flow diagrams indicate how an integrated design process would be carried out in practice. Readers should note that the full-size colour CAD/video outputs of these illustrations are much clearer than in these reduced black and white reproductions.

A Simulated Integrated Project

Simultaneous
aesthetic, performance
and
production
criteria assessment
for
alternative building design solutions
using
computer tools and techniques

image produced courtesy of owners

Computer videoimage of existing house

In the following plate section:

The first four plates symbolize the progression
of the four contributing co-designers' shared knowledge
application to each co-designer's basic data to produce
information that is exchanged to create the
final integrated information model on
a partnering basis.

The remaining plates simultaneously present
the definition and satisfaction of performance and
production criteria lists, in conjunction with the graphical
image when two options for development
are considered.

The simultaneous assessment of the two options
progresses from site to concept design options for both
the end-product and production process
of the proposed building solution.

The finally selected building solution, based on the client's
criteria priorities, then becomes part of the
school facility's existing integrated information model.

What has not been simulated, but can be imagined, given
available AutoCad third-party software systems, is greater
photorealistic exterior/interior material finish representation
and simultaneous structural, environmental
and quantity/cost analysis.

Simulation exercise by the author with B.N. and R.M. Noble.
Plates produced using AutoCad R12 with Adobe, MicroSoft Windows,
Harvard Graphics, Corel Draw and Asymetrix Packages

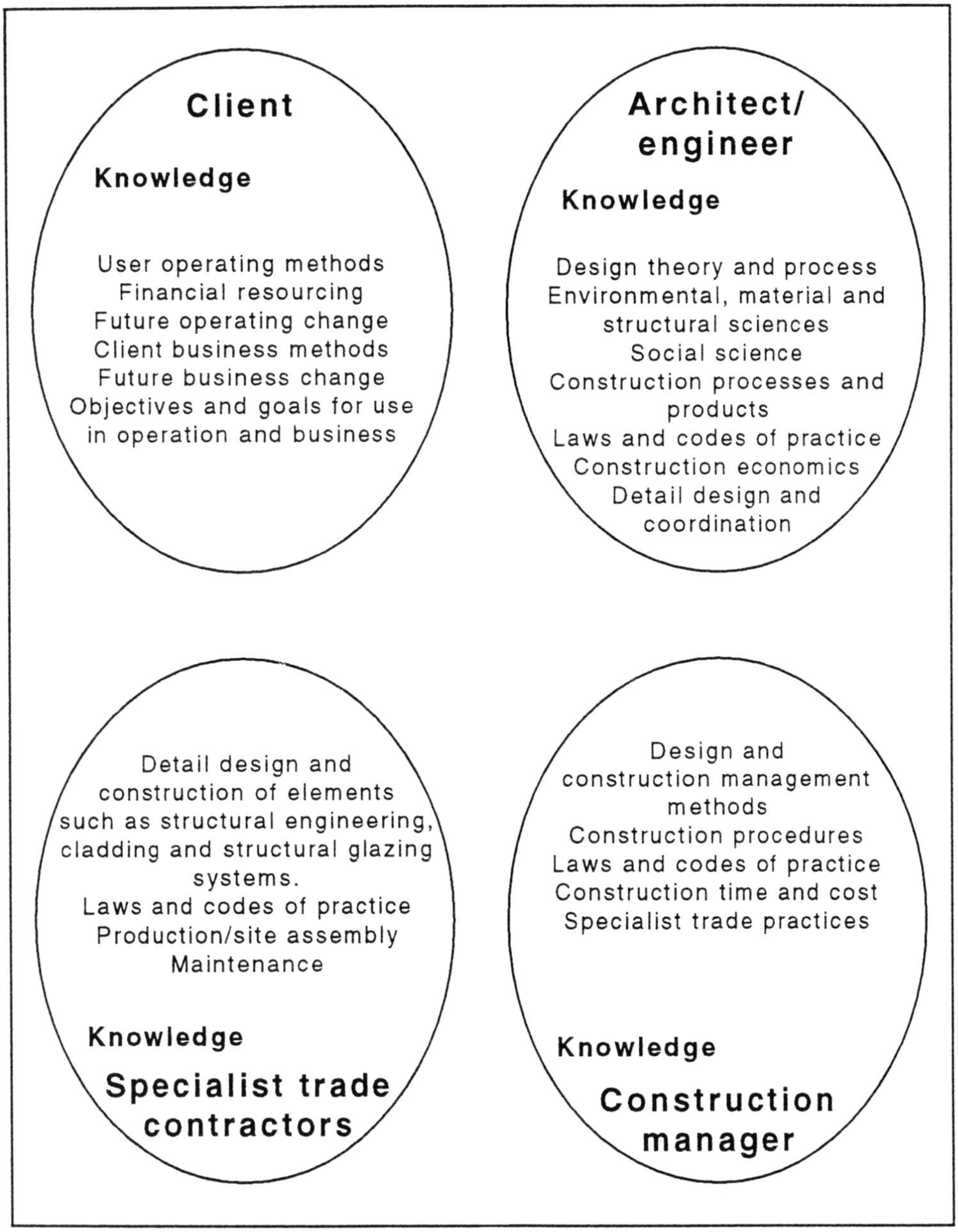

Co-designer's individual knowledge base

Client

Knowledge

Data

Aims and objectives
Requirements
•operating criteria
•building budget
•time scale
Benefit criteria

Weighting factors
Regulations and
codes

**Architect/
engineer**

Knowledge

Data

Use spatial sizes and
arrangement
Fabric/structure/services
Components and assemblies
Equipment
Appearance, style
Regulations and codes

Materials, components
Cost/rates
Assembly times/conditions
Availability, suppliers
Specialists
Equipment
Engineering fabrication methods
Regulations and codes
Data

Knowledge

**Specialist trade
contractors**

Cost/rates
Material movement and
storage
Plant
Suppliers
Specialist trade contractors
Subcontractors
Off site/on site assembly
methods
Regulations/codes
Data

Knowledge

**Construction
manager**

Co-designer's individual database

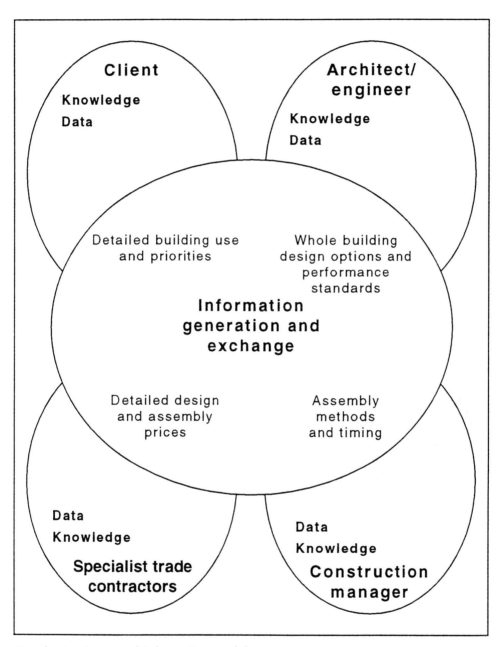

Developing integrated information model

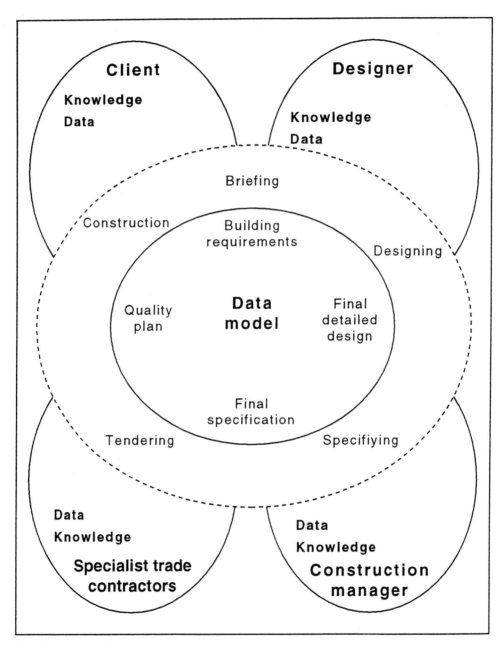

Final integrated information model

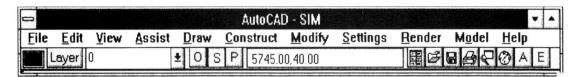

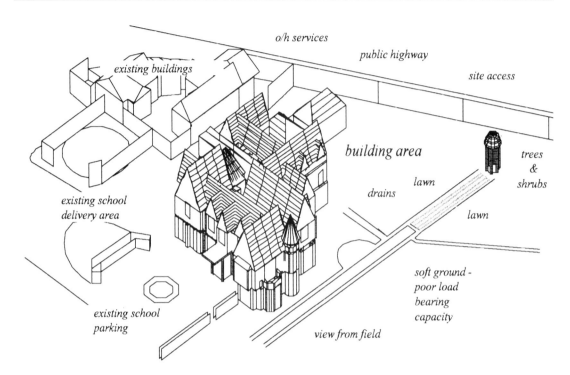

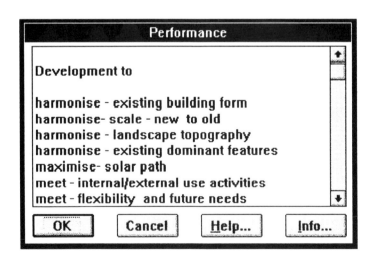

Existing site characteristics – critical performance criteria

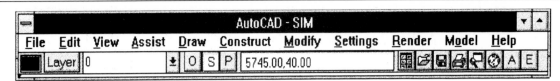

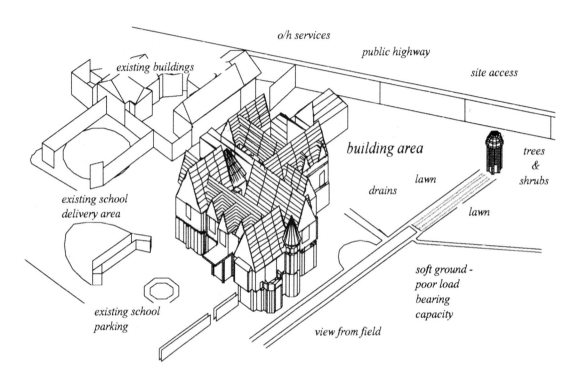

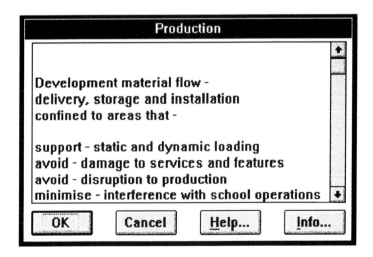

Existing site characteristics – critical production criteria

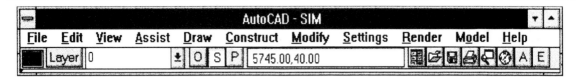

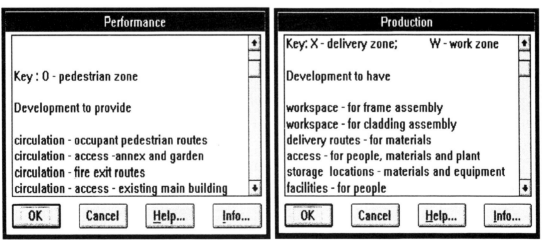

Existing site characteristics – critical production and performance flow criteria

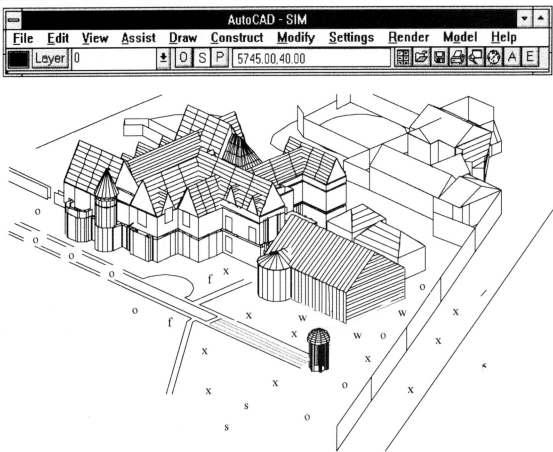

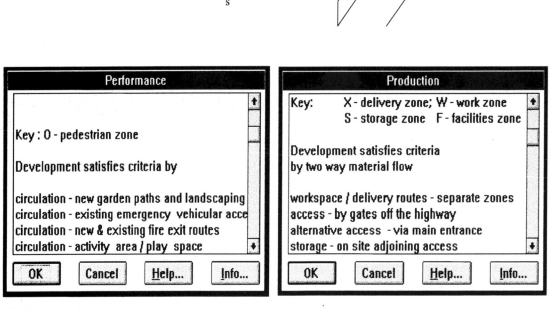

Site characteristics Option 1 – critical production and performance criteria satisfied

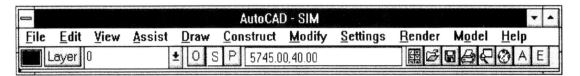

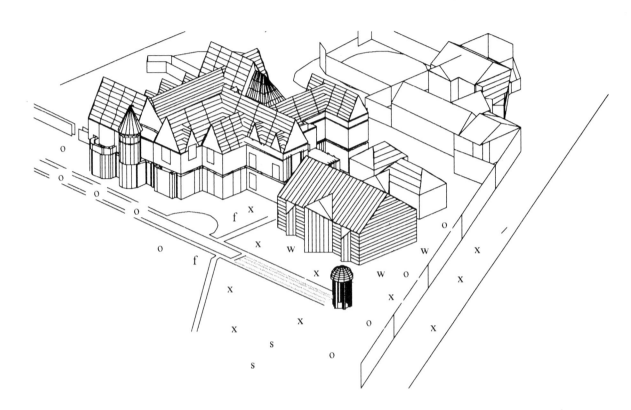

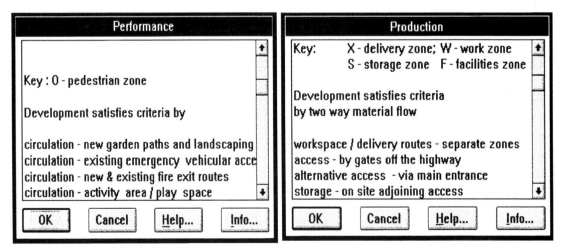

Site characteristics Option 2 – critical production and performance criteria satisfied

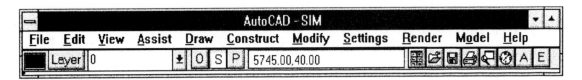

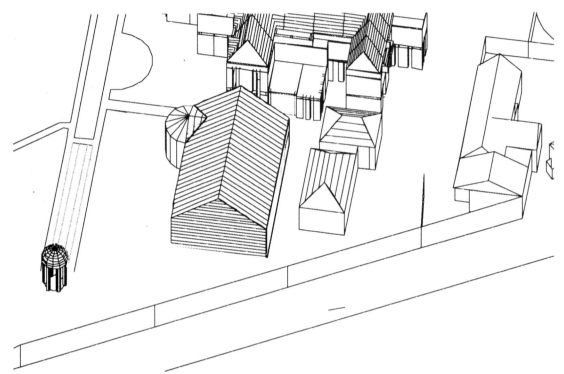

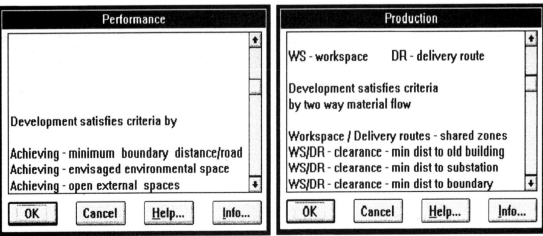

Site characteristics Option 1 – critical production and performance criteria satisfied

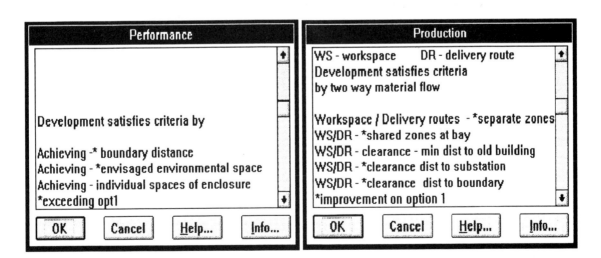

Site characteristics Option 2 – critical production and performance criteria satisfied

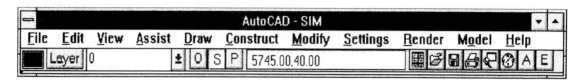

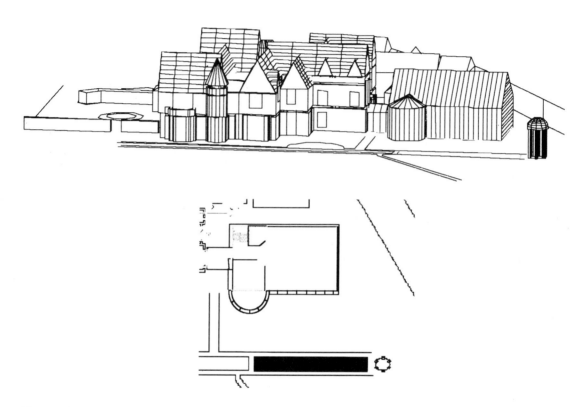

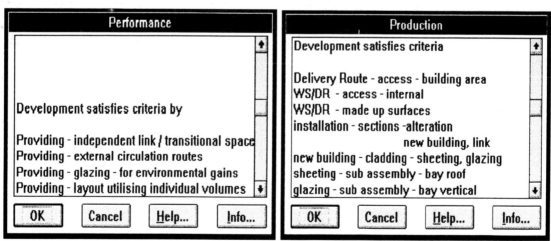

Site characteristics Option 1 – critical production and performance criteria satisfied

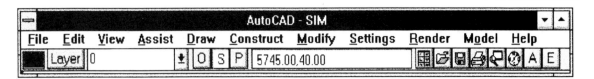

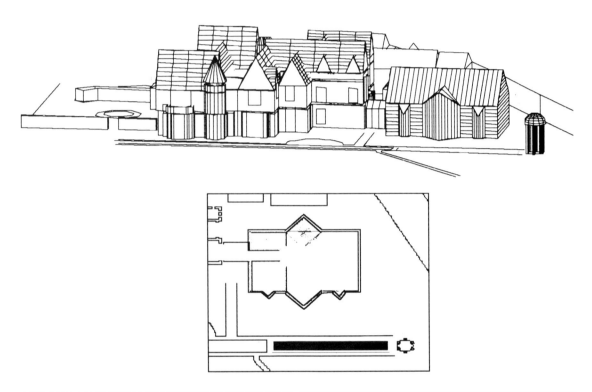

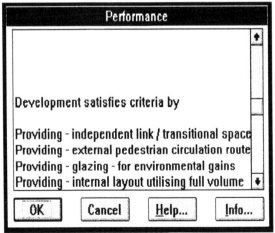

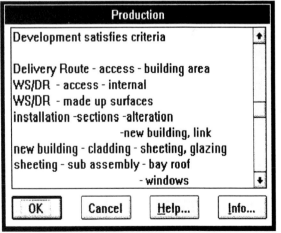

Site characteristics Option 2 – critical production and performance criteria satisfied

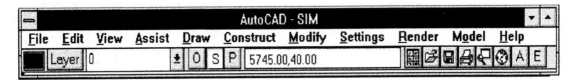

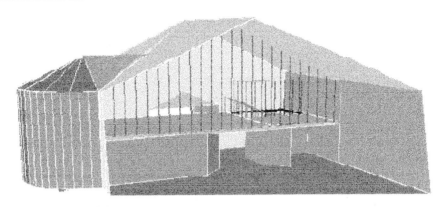

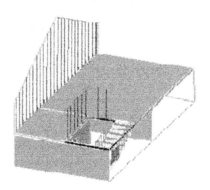

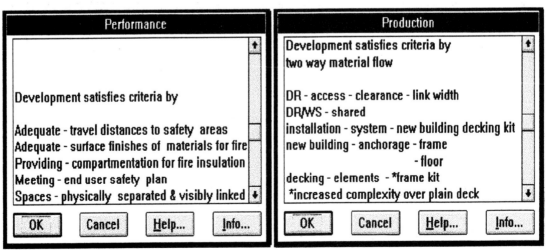

Interior Option 1 – critical production and performance criteria satisfied

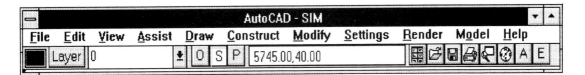

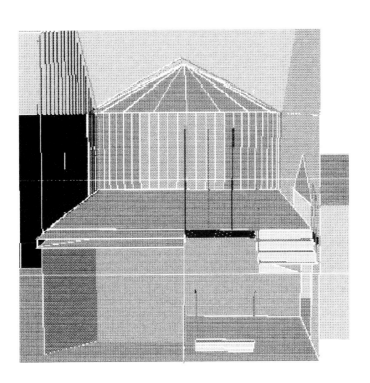

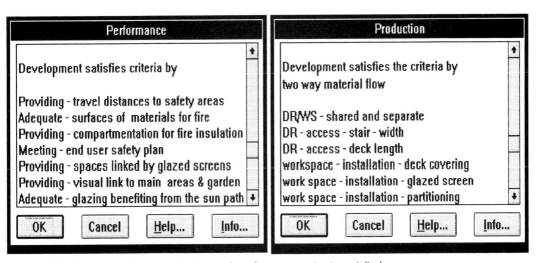

Interior Option 1 – critical production and performance criteria satisfied

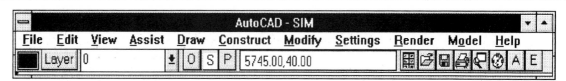

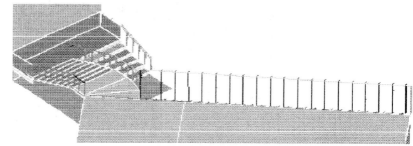

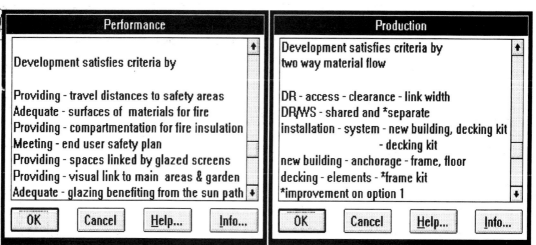

Interior Option 2 – critical production and performance criteria satisfied

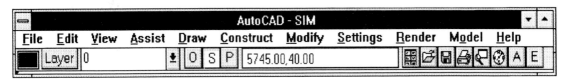

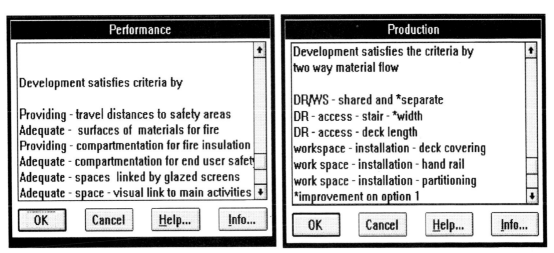

Performance	Production
Development satisfies criteria by	Development satisfies the criteria by two way material flow
Providing - travel distances to safety areas	DR/WS - shared and *separate
Adequate - surfaces of materials for fire	DR - access - stair - *width
Providing - compartmentation for fire insulation	DR - access - deck length
Adequate - compartmentation for end user safety	workspace - installation - deck covering
Adequate - spaces linked by glazed screens	work space - installation - hand rail
Adequate - space - visual link to main activities	work space - installation - partitioning
	*improvement on option 1

Interior Option 2 – critical production and performance criteria satisfied

image produced courtesy of owners

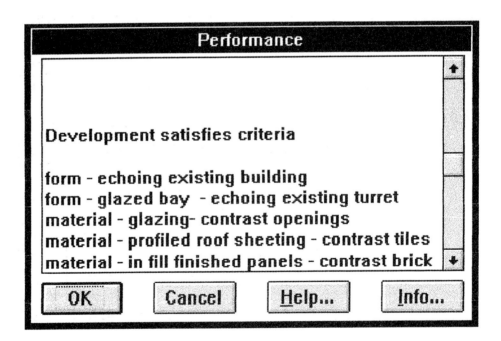

Video image of existing building blended with computer image Option 1

image produced courtesy of owners

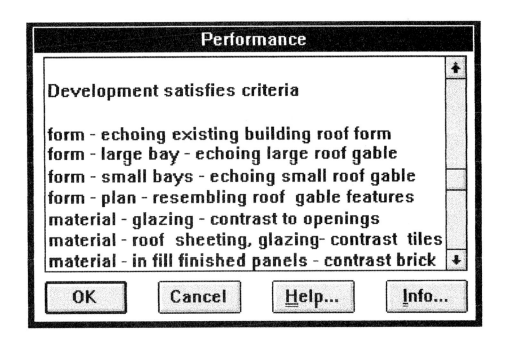

Video image of existing building blended with computer image Option 2

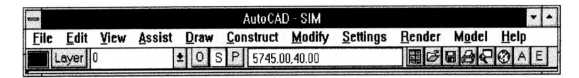

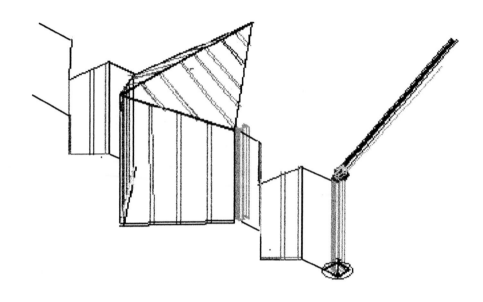

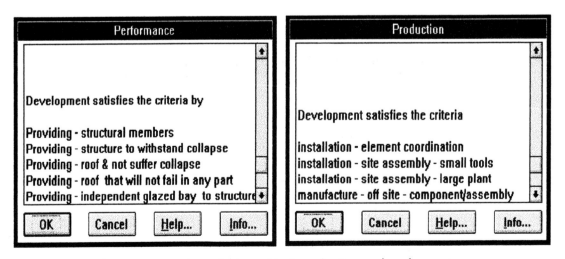

Schematic wire frame – corner bay glazing critical production and performance criteria satisfied

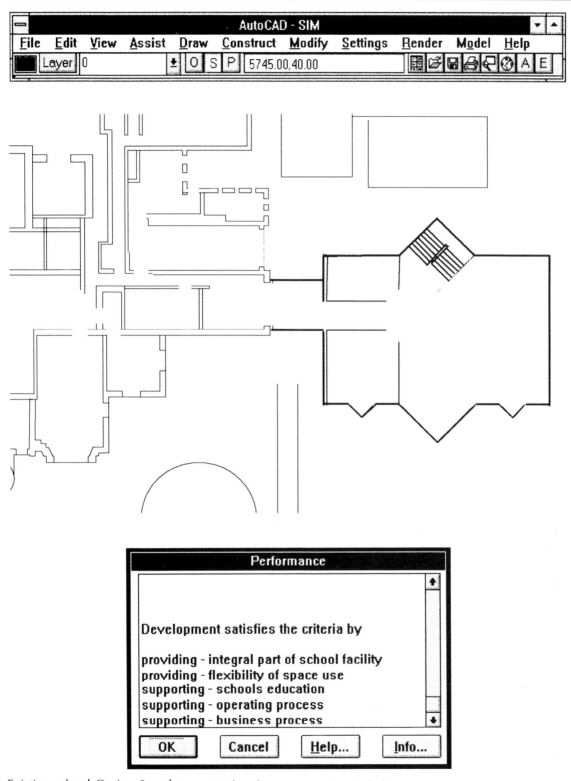

Existing school Option 2 – plan – critical performance criteria satisfied

ClarisWorks 1.0 - [P3.CWK [SS]]

File   Edit   Format   Arrange   Options   Window   Help

All schematic diagrams are to be considered as working plates and overviews as part of a complex sequence of procedures
and are to be considered in this context only
Plan based on "Partnering" method as opposed to traditional arrangements

Quality, Health and Safety Plan

Intended service life of the building	20 Years
Methodology for meeting the clients requirements	Acceptance criteria
Synopsis of the clients approved brief, including time, cost, quality requirements, a schedule of amendments	Brief Outline
Development of brief from principles to detail, providing for clients approval at points in time	Brief Detail
Examination, questioning & clarification of brief	Review
Identity of the client, or representative	Quality Plan
Principal staff should be suitably experienced and qualified	Quality Plan
Interface with others involved in the project	Commercial networks
Define responsibilities & duties of staff implementation adherence & design adequacy and verification	Quality Plan
Project Quality Manager / Planning Supervisor appointme	Health & Safety Plan
Project Programme	Time Duration/sequence
Consultation with clients representative & all other disciplines within design team	Meeting
Review findings	Report
Obtain clients approval at defined stages	Review
Retention of records for period	20 Years

	North	South	East	West	
Orientati	planning staircase	Activity Space	Activity Space	Art Room	
			Fire Exit	Computer Room	
Access	none	yes	yes	existing building	existing building linked to sanitary accommodation
Priority Design	single storey steel frame &		composite roof, wall decking & glazed walling		

	Month 1	Month 2	Month 3	Month 4	Month 5	Month 6	Month 7	Month 8	Month 9	Month 10	Month 11
Elements											
Design Temporary Works	**										
Foundations			**								
Slab			**								
Frame			**	**	**						
Roof Cladding						**					
Glazing/Cladding							**				
Finishes								**	**	**	
Practical Completion	date specified by client										**
1994 Price no inflation											
Apportioned Budget											
Payment as %	2.5	25	25	10	10	10	5	5	2.5	2.5	2.5
by client											

All prices and times confirmed by specialist trade contractors, construction manager, architect and engineer
Above Plan is not to be construed as a CDM Regulation Plan.
The concept option plates/diagrams are prior to any pre-project stages, appointments of various team members
and before any comparision of alternatives are undertaken

100

Time and quality requirements and achievements

Graphical outline of equipment to support communication between individual designers

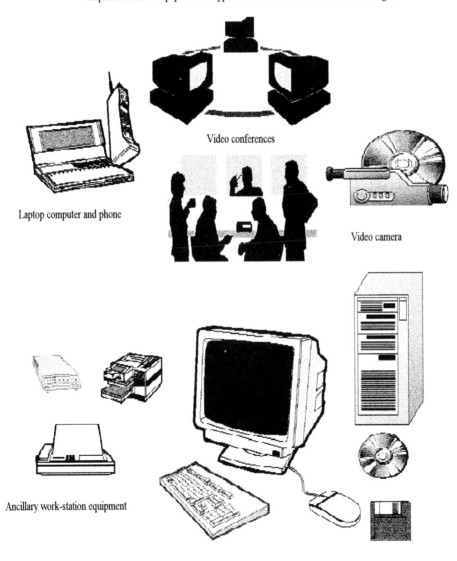

Video conferences

Laptop computer and phone

Video camera

Ancillary work-station equipment

Designer communication system

This simulation demonstrates that it is possible to carry out computer-integrated building design through a positively-managed project process using currently-available third-party software linked to a popular CAD graphics system. It also demonstrates where near-future improvement in CAD-related software is needed to make the process even more efficient and effective for integrated design.

The final outcome of this information management process throughout the briefing, designing, specifying and tendering phases of the project is an integrated information model which, with the inclusion of any necessary amendments required as a result of the actual construction phase, will be handed to the client on completion of the building.

This integrated information model will then be incorporated in the information model of the main building, being developed and based on an AUTOCAD system. The barn will then become an integral part of the overall school facility to be managed as the overall support of the school's education, care and staff training operating processes. This in turn is integrated with the school's overall business process of providing education and care service to the highest possible standard for the children, parents and placing authorities.

Summary

- The simulation has been limited in showing all the information integration and exchange that is now possible.
- The simulation assumes that a good partnering situation exists between the client, architect, engineer, construction manager and at least two of the specialist trade contractors.
- The simulation demonstrates that using even simple CAD-related systems information can be produced economically and exchanged between all those involved in a building project.
- The simulation demonstrates that the information generated for the design and construction of a building using CAD-related systems can then be used for its ongoing facility management.

Conclusions
for
practice

This book has been written to demonstrate the potential for integrating all the design processes involved in a building project using the emerging CAD-related computer-based tools and techniques. Even before these Information Technology (IT) tools and techniques are applied there needs to be a change in the procurement and management of the building project process itself. This change must affect the roles of the disciplines involved (including the client) and the relationships between them. The main aspect of this change should be that everyone involved (including the client) should see themselves and be seen by others as designers. Integrated design can only occur if each person's concepts about the building project solution are co-incidental as design is itself about conceiving change. In other words, if the building project design process is to be beneficially integrated then everyone needs to be of the same mind about the final building solution. That is the only way that everyone's needs – and not just the client's – will be met. But it is also the only way that clients' needs will be fully met, as the solution will be as much as a result of their own informed conception as that of any of the other project participants involved. One objective among many of integrated building design should be to cause clients to think seriously about their buildings.

Figure 9.1 shows that the finally-agreed 'solution' to the building 'problem' is truly the client's and that all the other project participants have been the enabling agents in reaching that solution.

The essential role that CAD-related computer-based systems will play in achieving this end will be through their capability for simultaneously processing and, more importantly simultaneously presenting, the many different and varied information aspects of an evolving building design solution. For example, when the

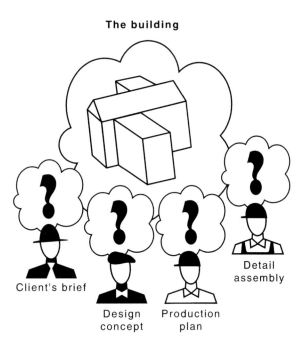

The building

Client's brief

Design concept

Production plan

Detail assembly

Fig. 9.1 The building solution – a product of one mind.

impact of a proposed building form and material upon building cost and operation duration and sequence can be immediately seen and understood, then agreed and collective design decisions can be made. This could apply equally in appreciating the relationship between building form and material and a particular facility management operation and many other fabric, structural or services design considerations. However, even with the most advanced IT tools and techniques, it would seem that the cycle of information processing would always have to start and re-start with the generation of a building form and material.

As many alternative building forms and materials can be generated easily, because of the drawing power of computers, so they can be quickly evaluated to see how all the building project requirements can be met simultaneously, due to the information processing power of computers. The 3D CAD graphics systems will therefore continue to provide the visualization medium but will now be a powerful front end and information integrating mechanism by which the knowledge of each participating designer can be brought together to produce an agreed solution.

Figure 9.2 shows that drawing (both as an activity and as a product) is not an end in itself but is a convenient mechanism to visually represent a condensed version of all relevant design information about a building.

So, if the power of IT, supported by improved process management, can bring about integrated design in building projects how will it affect the actual structure of the construction industry and its relationship with its client? In essence, very little, because each project participant will go on fulfilling their existing primary role. The difference will be in the way they can all work together to achieve an all-round satisfying solution to a building project. An improvement in their working together will be a result of the fact that the impact of one person's knowledge applied through their own designing on another's can be appreciated in coming to this solution.

Building form

Graphic information

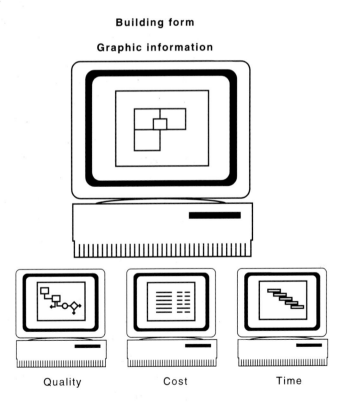

Quality   Cost   Time

Textual information

Fig. 9.2 The graphical image – a front end to the building information model.

Clients will go on requiring buildings, but will be in a better position to appreciate the overall design, cost and time consequences of the requirements of their project briefs. They should also be able to see how building can provide added value to their own operating process.

Architects will go on designing building forms and materials, but will be able to demonstrate the all-round consequences of alternative proposals better. They will (from the point of view of quality and risk management and future liability protection) be able to improve the ways in which they demonstrate the consequences of their architectural design decisions as they are being made. They will immediately, effectively and economically be able to exchange their information with all other disciplines to support interactive and common design decision-making. They will also be able to interactively verify any building form and material design proposal for the ever-increasing range of legal requirements with which they have to conform. Improved visualization techniques coupled with immediate displays of construction cost and time and operation-in-use implications will also give them assurance and confidence that their clients, as well as the other disciplines, fully understand their conceived building design proposals.

Engineers will go on designing the structures and services to support architectural forms, but will be in a better position to integrate their proposed solutions with those of the architect's for co-ordinated appraisal and verification.

Construction managers, replacing the traditional quantity surveyor and general contractor or as an extension of the architect's role, will be able to design and manage production systems for construction as an integral part to the architect's and engineer's building solution design process.

Specialist trade contractors will be able to apply their particular specialist rules for effective, efficient and economic design and production to evolving building form and material alternatives to provide specialist appraisal towards a finally agreed building design solution. They will also be able to be better assured that the information they have based their prices upon is exactly the same as the information they need to actually do their work.

One very practical consequence for all concerned is that what they have actually been contracted to do and priced for (be they architect, engineer, construction manager or specialist trade contractor) can be demonstrated to be the same as what is actually required in the building project. This should result in full expected payment and a greatly reduced risk of liability claims subsequent to the completion of the building design and construction process.

Figure 9.3 shows that design (both as an activity and as a product) must apply equally to the conception of the final building and to the production system through which it is to be realized.

Fig. 9.3 Designing the production system – an integral part of the building design process.

An additional benefit of computer-integrated building design is that the client receives not only the building but also an integrated information model with which to manage it as an ongoing facility. If this model contains not only the representation of the solution but also the reasons and consequences of change, then the model might even be said to be a knowledge-base. Whether it is owned by the architect or client or is shared remains an interesting question.

Finally, one essential change that must be made is the phasing out of the construction industry's traditional form of procurement. Despite the fact that it still accounts for 50% of all UK construction procurement (and much more in many other countries) as a project process system, it inhibits integrated building design. This is because it inherently assumes that the building design solution is completed before the designing contributions of the construction manager and specialist trade contractor are made. Integrated building design, with or without CAD-related computer-based systems, is only possible through the forms of procurement and management that allow and encourage the equal involvement of all the project participant designers during the building design process itself. The client-led, or even architect-led, construction management method is ideal. Design and build provides another alternative as long as the specialist trade contractor can make a direct contribution to the building design process in partnership with the architects and engineers. A complete partnering approach between the client and all other participants (particularly the specialist trade contractors who actually do most of the detail design and all of the physical production work) is perhaps the best method. This approach, supported by integrated CAD-related computer-based systems, would be the most ideal of all, if the 'most satisfying building solution' for a client's project is to be realized.

The greatest challenge of all from these emerging IT tools and techniques is to the architects themselves. Not in what they essentially do, which is to conceive of building forms and materials as solutions to building problems, but in their role and involvement in the building process. They are believed by many to be good at generating building design concepts, but not at managing the building project to meet the client's cost, time and technical standard requirements. The consequential threat from this belief could be that one day others will take the architect's 3B pencil sketch concept, computerize it and control all the subsequent information it will generate in order to manage the client's project to completion. This would relegate the architect to the equivalent of the automotive industry's stylist – a good living for the famous few but not for the lesser known many! The alternative scenario is a lot brighter. Making full use of these emerging IT tools and techniques and being the people who first conceive of the building form and material, architects themselves can lead the team of co-designers and then manage all the subsequent information to complete the client's project, and then maybe even use it to manage the resulting building as a facility in use.

Summary

■ Computer-based tools and techniques will make the possibility of integrated design in building a reality in the near future.

■ Changes in building project management, in which all other disciplines and clients are considered and act as designers, are necessary for the successful and beneficial application of these tools and techniques.

■ Computer-based systems will provide the client with a comprehensive record of both the process and product of the building design, which can then be used in ongoing facility management and any future alterations.

■ Architects should become the leaders of an integrated design partnership as the essential form-givers in a building project.

Simons
Construction –
computer-integrated
construction
for
quality
in
building

Background

Simons is a UK construction company based in Lincoln. It has long held a reputation for quality in its work and was the first building company in the UK to obtain registration to the BS 5750/ISO 9000 quality management standard. As part of its ongoing quality improvement process it has implemented a 'learning contractor' programme in partnership with several of its major clients, professional design teams and selected specialist trade contractors and suppliers. The aim of the programme has been to reduce the costs and time of construction, whilst maintaining the standard of quality through a systematic re-definition of its working methods.

With a staff of about 500 and an annual turnover in the order of £100m, the company is leanly structured with 'functional' directors and departments and site teams. In order to meet the increasing demands of construction clients it is undergoing a re-engineering of its total business process. This entails looking at the core activity of its business in order to identify what it actually is and then seeing how it can be done better, quicker and more cost-effectively. The result has been to take the view that the company has three essential areas to its business – key account management, production and technical services. A fourth area and the one that underpins and binds the other three together is Information Technology (IT).

Re-engineering – focusing on the client's project

The re-engineering approach encourages the company to see each task that is carried out in terms of the finished product of its business, that is to say the client's building project. IT becomes the practical means by which that approach can be accomplished in reality.

The approach is to manage the client's project through the process of production, based on the company's proven 'defined structure of customer relations' and gives the client a single point of contact throughout the life cycle of the project. A single manager manages the project from the point of enquiry through the bid, up to the placing of the order and on into the production process. Delivering the client's project becomes the prime process to control with the production team becoming responsible for the design, or completion of design if external architects are involved, production planning and management. The technical services provide the vital technical support to the production process by providing the general technical information to the project design and production team. Having the main aim to deliver the client's project on time, to cost and to an accepted quality standard means understanding and controlling the essential production process itself. A view of the production process, the emphasis on the process and not the project and the three constituent parts of production that represent the approach adopted by the company are shown in Fig. A.1.

Taking the three columns in turn, it can be seen that the left-hand column represents the application of knowledge to the production process, which comes from past projects or current project experience of the people involved. The central column represents the actual phases over time that the production process will pass through. The right-hand column represents information-related actions with outcomes to be carried out through the application of each person's knowledge.

It therefore follows that for the new approach to be successful:

☐ people must work in teams which constantly communicate
☐ the knowledge which they apply to communicate must be based on information which is both useful, timely and correct

Business Process Re-engineering

PRODUCTION

START

LEARN	Project launch	Transfer knowledge and information from KAM to construction team
DEVELOP	Develop contract plan	Rework based on construction information
EXECUTE	Procure resources in plan Execute work in plan	Plant, labour, materials and subcontract Cost, quality and programme
ANALYSE	Review success of contract	Profit (max value–least cost)/ resource performance assessment

FINISH

Fig. A1 A view of Simons Construction's production process.

□ the IT system must support these information objectives.

This must all ultimately support the company's business aim to have a satisfied client whilst making a profit.

The role of the Information Technology system

Information Technology is seen as an integral part of the company's business process system, supporting and linking the three main areas identified in its re-engineering approach. This position of its role in the company's view of itself will provide the ideal basis upon which to exploit the emerging computer-based technologies and systems. These will greatly improve the economic and efficient processing and exchange of information with added value each time it passes from one company process to another and externally.

So far, the way in which IT is being used specifically for production process improvement is as follows:

☐ For cost control. Improvements have been made through a greater degree of automatic cost information processing for valuations of stage payments from the client and to the sub-contractors/suppliers. Thus cash flow position and reconciliation between as estimated and actual expenditure are immediate and, when integrated with time and quality information in the future, the reason for the differences will be evident.

☐ For time control. Improvements have been made through a greater degree of automatic time information processing for setting the sequence and duration of trade contractor's work, ordering, and adjustment of resource levels that may be needed as a result of change.

☐ For quality control. Improvements have been made through a greater degree of automatic working method information processing for meeting particular design production requirements and, in the future, ensuring health, safety and environmental production risks have been identified in the design and planned for in construction.

It is envisaged that the company will shortly be able to integrate much of the above information with the CAD-generated building geometry (or their own or outside architect's design) starting to use the emerging tools and techniques described in Chapter 7. This will provide them with even more direct and immediate information exchange between design and their own production process.

All of the above improvements in production resource factor information representation, presentation and storage provide a more instantly accurate basis for people's knowledge application to decision-making. This is true not only for managing a current project but also for accumulating knowledge for planning future projects.

Conclusion

Simons see their construction business as one in which they must both cultivate and maintain satisfied clients through an increased partnership with external architects and specialist trade contractors. Information Technology is the means by which their own knowledge application in decision-making is currently supported. With information integration applications in the near future, improved knowledge acquisition and communication between all project participants within and without the company is expected to be achieved.

European
and
American
research
into
computer-
integrated
construction

Research into computer-integrated building design is currently being undertaken in major research projects both in the USA and the European Community. These projects are supported financially by both government and private industry as their outcome is considered to be of national importance. The view being taken is that as construction accounts for a high proportion of GNP, systems that will reduce its costs are in the national interest, which in the case of Europe, is the European Union interest. The beneficiaries of successful integration research are perceived as being:

☐ the computer system users, such as design and construction organizations who will have new 'tools' to enable them to exchange information more quickly and accurately, and so make their interactive working more efficient and economic;

☐ the computer system vendors who will be aware of information exchange needs and data exchange standards that are necessary for the future developments of CAD and CAD-related products;

☐ the clients and end-users of buildings who should benefit in the long term from better designed, constructed and maintained buildings as a direct result of integrated information models of buildings.

It is recognized by both researchers and practitioners that getting the computer to 'model' the semantics of interactive decision-making that is undertaken by human professionals in the building project process is a major task. Visions of automatic decision-making by the computer, the dream of earlier researchers, are still a long way from realization. They may not even be considered desirable, let alone practical. The common themes of such projects, both in the USA and in Europe, are now concerned with:

☐ how to ensure that data models remain consistent when building information is being transferred from one computer-based system to another;

☐ how to develop common international standards that vendors will eventually base their products on to ensure that data *can* be consistently exchanged;

☐ how to control data as it passes from one designer 'interest' to another in interactive computer systems; and

☐ how particular parcels of expert knowledge can be formulated and related to the CAD geometric 'dimensional' model in order to introduce some minor degree of intelligence in the computer-based design process.

Underlying all these projects is a concern for how such future information technology capabilities will affect the actual project process and the way in which the various 'traditional' professionals' working practices might be changed by them in the future.

A concern of the practitioners in these research projects is how these emerging information exchange methods, and their underlying conceptual models, truly reflect the practical information exchange needs of practitioners. This is a serious concern because unless the construction industry can see a real potential business benefit to integrated information exchange on projects there will not be a strong demand for 'integrating' CAD-related software systems and unless there is a user demand the software vendors will not produce the systems, because the development costs will present too great a financial risk.

Perhaps the greatest motivation for carrying out this research and development is the emerging demand by the construction industry's clients that all their project information is formulated and archived on computer. Clients are beginning to perceive that they will get better building quality and cost through the use of computers. Also the archived information model of a building's design and construction will provide a tool for their on-going facility management of the building's operation in use. The following projects are examples from those funded in Europe by the European Commission and those being supported by American industry and government over the last five years.

From Europe

Known by their acronyms, these projects are being developed with the financial support of different EC programmes. Their names, essential aims and the type and degree of information exchange that has been achieved so far in their development are described below.

ATLAS

The purpose of this project is to define a total methodology for computer-integrated large scale engineering (LSE) projects. It could also be applied to building projects. The work is based on a range of existing computer-based modelling tools and techniques. The research is being carried out under five separate but related work packages, as follows:

Work Package 1
This is concerned with establishing the formal basis for the development of open systems integration of the software to be used in the other Work Packages. The methodology builds on the way that the industry thinks, analyses and 'models' its working practices. It draws upon the idea that any production system that requires integration needs to be seen as a combination of the 'real' system, that is the actual construction process, and the 'information' system (the latter being the one that contains all necessary design and construction supervision processes). In order to use the information system to manage the real system a conceptual model of the latter is required. In ATLAS this is called the Project Reference Model. It extends to cover the maintenance, renovation, demolition and recycling stages of an LSE project. The reference model allows information to be exchanged using existing applications without significant modification. Shared information can be stored in a neutral format so that it

can be accessed by any application. Other information can be stored according to the 'view' of the particular application. The model follows the ISO/STEP standard.

Work Package 2
This is concerned with the current types of applications used in the engineering and construction industries and the possible information exchange between them. This is to be achieved by the applications accessing a real project model by either a direct file exchange via a neutral format or by direct access using a database 'query language' method. Information exchange has been achieved by importing 2D/3D files from a current CAD system and exporting them to an advanced object orientated AEC modelling system. This is illustrated in Fig. 7.10.

Work Package 3
This is concerned with the integration of emerging knowledge-based (KB) systems and the need to add more semantics to the basic model in order to facilitate knowledge as well as data exchange. The value of having direct access to these types of systems will be to give design engineers a wealth of knowledge based on collective experience. A neutral KB extension will be developed from the project model that will allow KBs to be directly interrogated by the central model within the computer. This will be achieved by the KB applications developing abstract information from the model according to the KB discipline view. The two KBs being experimented with concern archiving and retrieval of technical solutions of the whole or parts of projects and environmental or health and safety regulation checking.

Work Package 4
This is concerned with the development of an open framework environment to support the integration aimed for as the outcome of Work Packages 1, 2 and 3 with regard to the computer technology itself. This is to be achieved with an LSE Application Platform which will be UNIX-based and will comprise a configurable framework containing an artificial intelligence language of

the neutral LSE Project Reference Model and an object oriented database management system. It will follow STEP standards and support applications operating network-wide on multiple hardware platforms including PCs

Work Package 5
This is concerned with the management, demonstration and dissemination outcomes of the ATLAS work.

The ATLAS project has CAD vendor, national research organization and construction user companies from five EU member countries as its partners. The first phase of its work will be completed in 1995.

COMBINE 2

The purpose of this project was to establish a data infrastructure and tools for managing the information in a building design team, with the emphasis on the HVAC designer. The work envisages the development of future intelligent integrated building design systems (IIBDS) through which the energy, services and other performance characteristics can be analysed. This is based on the concept of separate designers sharing a common data repository. After building six design tool prototypes the current phase of the work concentrated on achieving information exchange using widely-available CAD systems to generate a building form. This has been done by exchanging CAD files, using the STEP standards, through a data exchange kernel (DEK) into the specialist design tools. Simple exchanges have been made and passed back to the DEK for re-integration with the CAD-generated model. The DEK has been implemented on top of a commercial object-orientated database and runs on UNIX and Windows platforms. On top of developing links to energy and services design systems, links were then developed with other information required in building design, such as component data bases, code documents and cost estimation.

The COMBINE project has universities and national research organizations from five EU member state countries as its partners and will be carrying out the important phase of testing the tools in practice during 1995.

CIMSTEEL

The purpose of this project was to improve the efficiency and competitiveness of the European structural steelwork industry through the application of computer-integrated manufacturing (CIM) techniques and the establishment of related standards. The project has developed the integration and interworking of ten structural engineering software applications which exchange information between 3D CAD steel framework models, assembly connections and structural calculations. Future work will be concerned with the exchange of information between the engineer's frame design and the steel component manufacturing process.

The CIMSTEEL project has 43, mainly industrial, participating organizations, from eight EU member countries and will be demonstrating its results on a real project for the wider acceptance of the developed methods and standards during 1995.

These projects have in common the support of the development and implementation of international data exchange standards and an object orientated data definition for CAD-related computer-based systems – through the application of STEP standards and supporting languages. This will ensure that in the future the integrity of information between one type of application and any one make to another will be maintained. However, at the time of writing, all involved would agree that we still have some way to go before this aspiration becomes a reality in day-to-day building design. They all also recognize the need to be able to utilise and build upon the readily available CAD and other related computer-based systems for both data and knowledge information exchange arrangements, as this will ensure their acceptance sooner, rather than later, and their incorporation into everyday practice.

Each of these projects demonstrates in different ways that meaningful information exchange is now possible between all the different knowledge domains used in the construction (large-scale engineering or building) process. This has been through the use of CAD-related computer-based tools and techniques that will gradually become available in commercial applications. The next research thrust related to all these projects is likely to be the demonstration of how computer integration will directly benefit the businesses of all the different design and construction organizations involved in the building process.

From the USA

The computer-integrated construction research being carried out in the USA is represented by the work of the Termin Institute's Center for Integrated Facilities Engineering (CIFE) at Stanford University, California. The Center's work is focused on process integration through the application of computer techniques as well as management methods, such as quality management and business process re-engineering. The applied research projects being undertaken are into applications that would relate to all construction projects ranging from process plants to buildings. The particular emphasis in the Center's work reflects the trends in American practice which seek to ensure the following objectives

☐ That the large corporate financial investments made by architectural, engineering and construction firms in their current CAD and CAD-related systems should be protected.
☐ The development of tools and techniques for integration using computers should make the best use of existing systems whilst overcoming the inherent problem of incompatible data representation.
☐ Exchange and sharing of information should enable complementary construction design and project management tasks to be carried out in a co-operative manner.

Meeting these objectives has resulted in an applied research and development approach which is similar in most cases to that of the European research projects. The current interest and work of CIFE can be seen in the programme of its autumn 1995 conference on 'Collaboration in the AEC Industry: Technology and Management Issues'. The subjects being covered can be categorized as follows.

Federated agent software architecture that permits collaborative working between individual software systems so that different designers can work on complementary tasks and communicate with each other over networks. The method was demonstrated through, on the one hand, a 'facilitator' that brokered requests, translated data structures and allocated resources and, on the other hand, through a peer-networking approach in which 'agent environments' directly communicated, creating a 'virtual work space'.

Object-oriented technology that facilitates the integration of 'incompatible' data from disparate software systems being used by individual project participants. The method helps to resolve the problems of multiple incompatible data structures in terms of information semantics, electronic formats, scope and level of detail. The approach ensures support for co-operative working whilst enabling individual designers to use the systems in which they have made considerable investment in both capital and training costs.

Internet working through developing commercial systems that allow project participants to access various business-related services and the impact of this method upon businesses and organizations. How computer-based systems can be used to support collaborative synchronous design over long distance Internet connections to support general design issues, brainstorming, forming architectural briefs, generating scheme design and 3D modelling. A further research outcome being presented concerns a prototype construction information server (CIS) which focuses on the electronic communication and dissemination of construction information – how CIS could be used for hypertext navigation, retrieval of documents, viewing of text, graphics and CAD documents and as an interface to E mail and other methods of communication.

CAD and CAD-related commercial software systems that control documents on multiple-site construction projects; that communicate ideas and plans quickly and accurately for validation during the innovative creative process; and that have the capability to interoperate with third party software applications are presented. The product development of the AutoCAD system is shown to be making advances in the degree of real-time document and model share, the desired level of interaction across applications, the control of information flow among different designers and the amount of raw data to be shared.

Conclusion

What is evident from both the European and American applied research and development into achieving computer integration for building in particular and construction in general are the amounts of human and financial resources needed. It can often be difficult to demonstrate the validity of the outcome of so much human effort and expenditure for the following reasons.

☐ What is actually 'seen' is what is normally 'seen' using former paper-based and dis-integrated computer-based systems. That is to say, the resulting graphical representations (or drawings) and alpha-numeric descriptions (or specifications, bills, programmes, method statements etc.) look the same!

☐ As the construction industry's main method of procurement, and consequentially its culture, is dis-integrated, with divided responsibility for design and construction, the benefits of integration itself are not immediately obvious to the design and construction organizations.

The next step in the development of the implementation of integrating CAD-related systems in practice requires a clear demonstration to the small to medium-sized design and construction organizations of the business benefits of such systems. Large organizations, aiming for mega-projects in their future business, already appreciate the benefits in terms of reduced costs, improved time and higher quality standards through improved information management and exchange. This is because, either as an organization or part of a project consortium, they will manage and control an integrated design and construction process. They may even also be managing the facility itself with the client/end-user leasing it from their organization or consortium.

However, small to medium-sized or organizations (even design organizations) may find themselves being employed as sub-contractor consultants to these large organizations. As part of the conditions of their appointment they may then be required to exchange their evolving design information interactively with the large organization employing them as the project proceeds. Their business motive for implementing the CAD-related integrating systems may then be to obtain work as this will become the 'normal' accepted method of working. However, being able to integrate their own project and business management processes through IT systems could also ensure that their sub-contractor status is well managed, the fulfilling of their contractual obligations clearly demonstrated – and thus they get paid without hassle!

Finally, two distinct outcomes are being generated from computer-integrated construction applied research and development in terms of available systems to practising designers and other construction professionals and clients. These are:

☐ Object-oriented and knowledge-based commercial CAD systems that will within themselves support the integration of design, construction and facility management processes. Examples of these are Reflex and ICAD, both of which in slightly different ways will enable various sets of rules to be encapsulated in order to generate or validate emerging design solutions of whole buildings or their elemental parts.

☐ Popular, and reasonably low-cost commercial CAD systems which are becoming object-based and for which third party software can be written to run in tandem to support integrated design, construction and facility management processes. An example of this is AutoCAD, the files of which can be exchanged with a range of systems which can be used to validate different aspects of the evolving design. The use of emerging STEP files will make that exchange even more useful and immediate as the CAD and other computer system vendors apply these standards to their future releases.

Each offers the possibility of appropriate systems according to particular procurement methods and organizational structures. The emerging networking, shared working and distant exchange of information over telephone lines increase the possibility of the integration of building design with people working in scattered, and even remote, locations.

A
training
programme
for
computer-integrated
construction

The need for a training programme stems from the importance of getting architects to alter the way they think about the use of CAD and CAD-related applications in design practice. Such a programme should both educate architects about project management opportunities and the need to model designs using computers, rather than just drawing designs using them, as well as train them in the use of the CAD-related system tools and techniques. The programme should also be affordable and attractive for practising architects timewise without interfering too much with their day-to-day business. It should also be aimed to encourage other co-designers (as proposed in this book), that is to say the client, engineer, construction manager and specialist trade contractor with whom architects work on building projects.

The following programme was designed initially to meet the above aims, but would need to be developed in detail with an industry-based steering group in order to ensure its viability.

The proposal has been described as an actual programme so that the aims and outcome of each day's training, and how these relate to everyday practice, can be appreciated. Although it is suggested as 'one day in' and then a return to the practice, this arrangement might not be practical. A balance would have to be struck between the needs of practitioners and the needs of the training staff. For the former, 'one day in' might be preferable, while for the latter 'three days in' might be preferable from the point of view of assimilation and application in the workshop setting.

Regardless of the final arrangement the following describes each day in content and what would be expected of the 'trainee' once back in the practice. This I have described as homework.

Computer-integrated construction: a training programme for architects working with engineers, specialist contractor designers, cost and construction managers and client's facility managers

BACKGROUND

Computer-based tools and techniques that will support building design integration will soon be readily available in practice. This means that a CAD-based data model of a proposed building can be created as it is being designed by the architect. This model will contain all the critical information about the building's engineering and construction and future management as a facility. During the design development process the architect will be able to continually verify the design against a range of engineering designs, specialist contractor designs, cost and construction management and client's facility management criteria using CAD-linked software packages.

The availability of these tools and techniques will bring about a desirable change in the construction industry's practice which will allow the simultaneous design, engineering and construction of buildings. It will also allow the architect to demonstrate directly to the client the all-round impact of architectural design decisions as they are being made. This should greatly improve the communication between all the participants involved in a building project in order to achieve the time, cost and quality targets.

AutoCAD, with its wide-ranging third-party software and developing data interchange capabilities, provides the ideal computer system for training architects in this new method of practice. Architects can be trained to use the CAD system as a design modelling tool, rather than just a drafting-for-visualization tool. This will support their interaction with the engineers, construction managers and client's facility managers. Project management methods will also be included in the training programme to ensure that computer modelling becomes an integral part of the total project management process.

THE PROGRAMME

The aim of the training programme will be to use as much hands-on simulation of the interactive building design process as possible. This will be achieved through the creation and exchange of CAD building design information by the architect with the engineering, construction management and facility management databases. The tutors will be experts in building modelling, management and the use of current CAD and related software systems. The timing will spread the delivered programme over an approximate 12 month period to allow gradual assimilation into the supporting architectural practices between the teaching days as 'homework' for those attending the course and developing the skills.

Day 1
Introduction to computer-integrated building design as a new approach to architectural practice; modelling tools and techniques for building design; and the current CAD-based standardized conventions that support data exchange.

Homework
Review own practice's position for introducing the new approach.

Day 2
CAD generation of outline building forms as data models that can exchange information with other databases; use of standardized conventions in CAD to support the required data exchange; supporting project management methods for building design, construction and facility management.

Homework
Review own practice's methods and changes required to adopt this approach to their current use of CAD during the building design process.

Day 3
Methods of 'rule base' analysis by engineering, cost and construction management and client's facility management database systems of CAD-generated outline building forms; supporting project management methods for the early design development stages of the building project.

Homework
Review own practice's methods of working and changes required with engineers, cost and construction managers and client's facility managers using CAD-linked systems during the building design and construction management processes.

Day 4
CAD-generated detail design for structural engineering elements as data models for information exchange with structural engineering 'rule-based' systems for design verification; use of standardized conventions in CAD to support the required data exchange; supporting project management methods for working with structural engineers.

Homework
Review own practice's methods of working and changes required with structural engineers using CAD-linked systems during the building design process.

Day 5
CAD-generated detail design for services engineering elements as data models for information exchange with services engineering 'rule-based' systems for design verification; use of standardized conventions in CAD to support data exchange; supporting project management methods for working with services engineers.

Homework
Review own practice's methods of working and changes required with services engineers using CAD-linked systems during the building design process.

Day 6

CAD-generated detail design for fabric elements as data models for information exchange with specialist contractor 'rule-based' systems for building production design verification; use of standardized conventions in CAD to support the required data exchange; supporting project management methods for working with specialist contractors.

Homework

Review own practice's methods of working and changes required with specialist contractor designers using CAD-linked systems during the building design process.

Day 7

CAD-generated building forms and detail as data models for information exchange with cost and construction management 'rule-based' systems for building cost and time verification; use of standardized conventions in CAD to support the required data exchange; supporting project management methods for working with cost and construction managers.

Homework

Review own practice's methods of working and changes required with cost and construction managers using CAD-linked systems during the building design process.

Day 8

CAD-generated building forms and detail as data models for information exchange with client's facility management 'rule-based' systems for building operation-in-use verification; use of standardized conventions in CAD operation to support the required data exchange; supporting project management methods for working with the client's facility managers.

Homework
Review own practice's methods of working and changes required with client's facility managers using CAD-linked systems during the building design process.

Day 9
CAD-generated building forms and detail as data models for information exchange with building code and regulation 'rule-based' systems for good practice verification; use of standardized conventions in CAD to support the required data exchange; supporting project management methods for working with building regulators.

Homework
Review own practice's methods of working and changes required with building regulators using CAD-linked systems during the building design process.

Day 10
CAD-generated building forms and detail as integrated design data models for managing the construction stage of the building project for design change control and construction monitoring; supporting project management methods using CAD-linked systems during the building design construction management process.

Homework
Review own practice's methods of working and changes required with construction managers using CAD-linked systems during the building construction process.

Day 11
CAD-generated building form and detail as integrated design data models for managing the operation-in-use stage of the building project for facility management and refurbishment design monitoring; supporting project management methods for working

with facility managers using CAD-linked systems during the building operation-in-use process.

Homework
Review own practice's methods of working and changes required with client's facility managers using CAD-linked systems during the post-occupation period.

Day 12
CAD-generated integrated design data models as the basis of architectural practice business management support using CAD-linked business systems for building projects; review of course and implications for change in architectural practice.

The programme will be carried out in a CIC studio with networked CAD PC-based workstations in order to simulate working in shared data space – the way in which architects and their co-designers will soon be working. A large-screen CAD system on which each individual's CAD 'outcome' was integrally-demonstrated using Windows is also seen to be essential equipment for such a studio. The homework and breaks between training days (whether they are single or multiple 'days in') would ensure that what is learnt is immediately fed back, tested and reviewed in the workplace.

Conclusion

The overall aim of this type of training programme should be to create a simulation of a 'shared working environment'. The skills and knowledge to be acquired are those that will enable practitioners to adopt new 'co-operative' working methods, both through using the emerging computer technology, as well as the developing process management methods for construction projects. The skills and knowledge of one without the other will achieve little in ultimately improving working practice in the construction industry.

Setting
up
the
computer-integrated
construction
practice

The foundation of people working on building projects in the construction industry is the single trade operative during the construction process and the individual architect or engineer during the design process. While the operatives actually build, the architect and engineers design what the others build. All the other people involved in the project are controlling, coordinating or communicating this fundamental work of the individuals who build and design.

Whether the individual architect or engineer operates in a one-person design practice or a small, medium or large design organization, he or she is the basic 'people working unit' in the creative design process. The individual, using experiential knowledge, makes design decisions as the project evolves from the beginning of the briefing phase through, and often into, the construction phases of the project. Those design decisions then have to be validated by being exposed to other people's opinionated 'experiential knowledge' and other generally available and relevant construction information. CAD-related computer-based systems, when networked and using shared 'data space', put the individual architect and engineer in the same position, with the same available method of working whether he or she operates as part of a large organization or as a one-person practice. That is to say, they can now carry out their work in conjunction with others using computer system links, and in essence it makes no difference whether those links are short- or long-distance, within the same location or between separate locations.

The following example of a one-person practice in terms of facilities, equipment, methods, skills/knowledge and performance standards illustrates the smallest 'design unit' (a term used in a currently developing British Standard Guide to Managing Design in the Construction Industry) that would always exist in any building project. This 'design unit' is then taken to be applying

CAD-related computer-based integrating tools and techniques to its work.

The facility – the 'office' seat for a paperless process

The changing workplace, particularly the office, is a feature of all modern organizations whose prime function necessitates that their employees work with information. The gradual, and now accelerating, move from paper-based to IT-based systems, whilst not yet producing the predicted 'paperless' office, means that:

☐ work takes place at computer seats rather than office desks;

☐ the passing of information from one worker to another in order to carry out further work becomes the transfer of a dynamic digitized data rather than a paper document;

☐ reviewing information output from one's own or other people's work becomes the study of a textual or graphical screen image rather than the study of a textual or graphical paper document, and with a Windows environment, it is possible to review different textual or graphical images simultaneously; and

☐ storing information output to await further input or if completed, archiving without the need for filing cabinets.

The integrating IT facility is therefore one which needs only a seat for work even though other space is still needed for face to face meetings and general socializing between those who work together. Even table space for the collective viewing of paper documents can be replaced by large-screen systems, video-linked to the individual workstation seats. This equipment, however, only needs to be located with the lead designer/project manager who will be ensuring that all design contributions are leading to a commonly agreed 'solution'.

The equipment – the 'front end' to a wider world

The basic specification for an IT system to be used by the individual architect or engineer as designer in a building project would be as follows:

- [ ] a 486 DX (or faster)
- [ ] an LCD, 15, 17 or 20 inch monitor (or similar) with a suitable graphics card
- [ ] RAM, floppy, hard disk, CD ROM, tape or similar data storage device combinations to suit the system
- [ ] a mouse or digitizer or another pointing device and software
- [ ] a scanner and software
- [ ] a video camera, video capture card, sound card, speakers and software
- [ ] a fax/modem and software
- [ ] a printer/plotter
- [ ] a phone, phone line and software
- [ ] an operating system supporting a Windows-type environment
- [ ] AEC software supporting shared information with external data sources, the designer's additional software and shared information media between designers using different AEC packages
- [ ] a general integrated database, spreadsheet, word processor and graphics software.

Although it would not be appropriate to list the various costs of this equipment here, it can be said with confidence that the prices of the above components will fall in time. That is to say, having this equipment will become economically viable and, in terms of winning business, it will be financially disadvantageous not to have it. It would be equally inappropriate to suggest that for an 'integrating' practice any of the above systems could be prioritized, for to achieve 'integration' in the widest possible sense all parts are equally important.

Finally, it could be argued that in a large organization of *designers* who are in effect 'under the same roof' and close, the cost of individual seats would be no less than for the individual practitioners operating from remote locations. This is due to the fact that the power required at each seat would need to be as great as possible because of the sheer volume of data being transmitted and processed. A 'server' and 'slave' configured system, in which only the server had the CAD-related systems and the slaves used them, would very rapidly reach its practical working limits.

The method of work – a 'continuous consultation' with others

It has long been argued and can be observed from practice that the architect's (and to a lesser extent engineer's) actual work as a designer comprises the 'processing of information'. Although the creative thought for a building design solution may come quite rapidly from inner knowledge and inspiration by the individual, this action is always likely to be:

☐ preceded by the gathering of a multiplicity of information from a variety of diverse documented sources and people in order to arrive at the basis of the inspiration; and
☐ followed by the gathering of a multiplicity of information from a variety of diverse documented sources and people in order to validate the inspired solution against the actual requirements of the client's brief, legislation and compliance with good practice standards.

Therefore the need to consult during the design process is paramount to ensure that inspired thought will in fact result in a solution that demonstrably meets all the requirements. It could be argued that in the light of experience the more continuous this consultation can be the better. Otherwise the designer may rapidly become committed to a solution that, as a result of further consultation may have to be seriously amended or rejected altogether. For example, a proposed conceptual form and material for a building cannot simply be made to meet the client's construction budget when detailed production issues are finally considered.

The timing and information content of every consultation becomes critical in the validation stages of each step of the evolutionary design process. The information may need to come from another co-designer, based on their knowledge, or a source document regarding some good practice or regulatory aspect of a particular type.

The integrating IT systems will therefore both offer and ultimately demand a method of working that comprises the sharing of knowledge through the exchange of meaningful information on a continuous basis.

Skills and knowledge – the 'expert generalist' in design information

The skills and knowledge required and applied by architects and engineers as designers using integrating IT systems will by and large be those that are needed in paper-based approaches. The range of understanding of social, economic, scientific and aesthetic subject domains of knowledge needed for, in particular, the architect will be those required by, for example, the EU Architect's Directive. However, the practicalities of day-to-day architectural practice mean that only a very high level of these 'knowledge' areas can be held within the individual architect's own mind. Such knowledge can only be accessed through other documented or another expert's personal 'information' as and when necessary during the design process.

The expertise of the architect is therefore in having both the skills and knowledge concerning the additional 'information' he or she needs at a particular time and where that information may be found. As important is knowing when it needs to be accessed and used at each critical stage in the evolutionary design process.

The further skills and knowledge now required by the architect using integrating IT systems must therefore be concerned with these systems themselves. First, they must know exactly how they will be able to access and apply specialist 'information' in a meaningful manner from any of a variety of general and specific project sources, be they expert people, expert knowledge or databases. They require the skills to use the IT systems which are described above. These will not be simply CAD systems, with which many architects are now familiar, but the CAD-related software systems needed to analyse the evolving design as well as those, such as Email, Internet and data sharing systems that will all be needed simultaneously to support co-operative working through IT.

The integrating IT systems will therefore both expand the architect's general architectural 'knowledge' for design, and will demand new knowledge and skllls to access and apply this expanded knowledge through the emerging IT systems themselves.

Performance standards – 'right first time'

The need for efficient, effective and economic work by the construction industry's designers (as their fees are constantly being reduced) must result in a 'right first time' approach to their design activities. The performance standard in terms of 'information' as an input to any design task in any stage of the evolutionary process must be that the information is immediately retrievable, represented in the correct data structure and presented in the appropriate format to the user.

Integrated IT systems, in which CAD images are in fact the representation of real objects with usable attributes for any particular cost, time or performance analysis, enable the designer to both give and receive information presented appropriately. The capability of converting 'object data' from one format to another, either in alpha-numeric or graphical form means that the information can also be immediate. It is therefore the emerging IT systems themselves that become the essential process that ensures that the information input to any design task is not deficient in either form, content or timing.

Conclusion

The design organization can become the organization of a process of collaboration between individual designers. Given that all project participants are now considered as co-designers (as proposed in Chapter 4), linked CAD-related integrating systems all provide for a co-operative design process and agreed solution. The individual designers can be remote or next door to each other – their location makes no difference. When they need face-to-face discussions they can even be connected by videophone or, from time to time and for social reasons, come together to meet in person. And that meeting place does not even have to be one of the organization's traditional types of office.

Epilogue:
Working
in
2001?

The architect, working at his or her CAD station and electronically linked to other co-designers (which now include the client and construction manager) generates alternative building forms and material concepts. Immediate access to cost, time and performance standard data, as well as regulations and standards, gives immediate feedback on how targets are being met. Evolving into greater detail, the architect's design becomes understood by everyone so that with each iterative and evolutionary step it becomes a commonly agreed 'solution' to the building project 'problem'. Continuous consultancy replaces periodic presentations so that all design choices are understood, agreed and, for feedback, archived. The power of graphics is fully utilized to ensure that all the implications of choice are communicated – for example using changing colours for heat-loss differences, changing shapes for cost and time differences and animation to visualize both building use and production activities. Business administration processes are automatically accounted for as each person's work contribution uses up their own time, cost and energy resources. The completed information model is then carried forward to control construction, updated if changes occur, and finally passed to manage the completed building as a facility that supports the client's business.

The total project process is now under control without architectural creativity and innovation being impaired!

Bibliography

The following list of references comprises a selection of books, conference papers and research projects, all of which have contributed to my view of the development of computer-integrated building design in practice. They are listed chronologically to show an evolution in both my thinking and other work that has contributed to the subject. A brief description of their significance is given.

1960   *Vitruvius, The Ten Books of Architecture,* translated by Morris Hicky Morgan, Dover Publications Inc., New York.
Takes architects back to their Roman roots and demonstrates that today's separate practice of 'construction project management' was included in yesterday's practice of 'architecture'. Does not mention computers but interestingly enough does not mention the word design either, presumably because architecture then was all about creating buildings, while the separation of their conceptualization and realization as different activities and responsibilities was not even considered.

1973   *Design in Architecture,* Broadbent. G., John Wiley, Chichester (revised 1988).
A standard work from the 1970s (recently updated) that describes in some depth the various methods and techniques for design as an activity and process and how it is applied in the practice of architecture. A process for building design proposed that allows a systematic evaluation of how alternative proposals might satisfy different design criteria priorities. Ways in which computers may be applied in the future to the architectural design process and how the best use might be made of the human designer and the computer as a support are discussed.

1975   *Spatial Synthesis in Computer-Aided Building Design,* Eastman. C. (ed.) Applied Science Publishers Ltd, London.
A standard work from the 1970s in which it is suggested that architectural design is essentially a spatial synthesizing problem that could be addressed by systematic and formal methods of space sizing and arrangement. Computer-based CAD-related approaches are proposed to

aid designers in coming to spatial solutions to buildings. It also gives early examples of AI language approaches that represent knowledge in the computer in order to generate or evaluate solutions proposed by the computer.

1977 *Information Methods for Design and Construction*, Paterson. J., John Wiley, Chichester.
Proposes the view that architectural design is primarily concerned with processing a great deal of information about the various construction and in-use performance aspects of buildings. Contains a description of the experience of very early applications of computer-integrated design during the 'system building' period of local authority architecture in the UK. The production design drawings generated in 2D CAD could automatically create the construction resource costs from a pre-defined constructional method.

1980 *How Designers Think*, Lawson. B., The Architectural Press Ltd, London.
This addresses the deep issue of design as a human intellectual activity with regard to the work of architects. It puts computers in their rightful place as providing support to the human activity and describes the evolutionary and iterative nature of the design process itself.

1980 *Architecture and the Micro-Processor*, Paterson. J., John Wiley, Chichester.
Another book from the author of *Information Methods for Design and Construction* which discusses many issues regarding architecture itself and its place in society. Patterson suggests how the growing power of micro-computers would one day have a great impact on the way architecture is practised and realized. Some of these predictions are now becoming possibilities with both the improvements in computer technology and pressures on the architectural profession to change from clients and the wider construction industry.

1985 *Computer-Aided Architectural Design Futures*, Pipes, A., (ed.) Butterworth, London.
This comprises the conference papers of reports about many research projects going on in Europe and elsewhere during the early 1980s into the applications of computers as aids to architectural design. This work ranged from modelling the various processes involved and developing experimental applications using artificial intelligence (AI) techniques, improvements in CAD imaging and methods of integration.

1986   *ESCAD '86 Workshop*, Cornick, T., Bull, S., Nowell, M., Coles, E.J., University of Reading, Reading.
This is a report on the current research being undertaken in UK construction research institutions into the application of expert systems and issues surrounding knowledge elicitation and representation. It covers the research being carried out into a range of 'knowledge domains' used in the building design and construction process and includes the author's own BERT which linked an AutoCad image to an expert system for automatic evaluation of the detail design of a drawn brickwork elevation.

1986   *Architectural and Building Design: An Introduction*, Young, W., Heinemann, London.
A practical guide to architectural practice and the building design process for young architects. Categorically states that the value of computers is in the 'evaluation' step of the building design process and that the creativity of architects to generate designs will go on outside the computer.

1988   *CAAD '87 Futures*, Maver, T. and Wagter, H., Elsevier, Oxford.
Describes much of the same type of research being carried out in the report of the 1986 conference, two years on. Contains reports on a variety of expert system application research projects being undertaken around the world. This demonstrated that there was no problem in creating an expert system for any aspect of building design or construction – the main problem would be in interrelating them for a whole building design within a CAD-related computer-based system.

1988   *The Telling Image*, Davies, D., Bathurst, D. and R., Clarendon Press, Oxford.
Describes and discusses the power of computers for communication in all fields of human activity, especially the powerful impact of the use of graphics in communicating all types of information. It is deduced that CAD imaging will remain the focus in applying computers to building project design information.

1988   *Quality Management – Reducing Avoidable Costs in Construction*, Cornick, T., Teaching Company Programme, Kyle Stewart Ltd/University of Reading, Reading.

This was an applied research project completed in 1992, comprising a series of investigations into various design and production process improvements as a development of a design and build company's registration to BS/EN/ISO 9000. One of the many outcomes was the identification of the need to integrate information on construction cost control and construction estimating and planning through company-wide IT systems. Another was the need to control evolving detail design for cost once a construction price had been given in a design and a bid accepted by a client.

1989   *The Age of Unreason*, Handy, C., Arrow Books Ltd, London.
A view of the future of living and working based on an extrapolation of what is happening now in terms of the social and economic frameworks of business organizations. The change is predicted to be discontinuous and the requirement of 'upside down thinking' necessary to survive. The rapid evolution of IT is seen as one of the main agents of that change. Architectural practice, and the way clients see and procure buildings as part of their rapidly changing businesses, will be no exception to the implications of these events.

1990   *CIB W74/78 Seminar – Designing for Production*, Cornick, T. and Noble, B., Seminar Proceedings, Tokyo.
A paper that describes the outcome of research into how the activity of design should be considered as generating both the end-product and production system of a building. This was based on the fact that the essential generic information required to evaluate the building's 'operation-in-use' satisfaction was the same as that required to evaluate the building production satisfaction. This was a useful conceptual basis on which to develop integration approaches using computer applications.

1990   *Information Management for the Construction Industry*, Wix, J. and Cornick, T., NEDO Data Exchange in Building Committee, London.
A publicly-available document that comprehensively describes the needs and methods of information exchange between all the participants in a construction project. Based on past and current applied research into all the construction management and computer-based data exchange requirements it provided one of the major informed outcomes of the work of the above committee.

1991   *Construction Management Forum – Report and Guidance*, Centre for Strategic Studies in Construction, University of Reading, Reading.

A publicly-available report that describes the deliberations and outcomes of leading construction industry practitioners on the management approach to procuring building projects. Provides very practical guidance on how the construction management method of procurement should be undertaken and stresses the importance of the client's full and positive involvement in the design process. It identifies the exact functions of and relationship between the key participants in a building project and the way in which communication supports the successful working of those relationships.

1991   *Quality Management for Building Design*, Cornick, T., Butterworth-Heinemann, Oxford.

Describes the result of research into applying the principles of quality management on the building process, particularly to the early design phases of a project. It proposes a task/phase 'model' for managing quality, and its improvement, throughout six phases of a building project. It also stresses the importance of the fact that it is information that is the vital 'chainlink' for managing quality throughout the project between the client, designer and construction manager.

1991   *International Construction Project Management*, Bennett, J., Butterworth-Heinemann, Oxford.

This book comprehensively describes a range of project management models for construction and the roles and relationships of the project participants. It concentrates on methods of managing the construction project and stresses the importance of communication, which information exchange must support, for successful project management.

1991   *The Essence of Information Systems*, Edwards, C., Ward, J. and Bytheway, A., Prentice Hall, London.

This is one of a series of guides to the 'essence of management' which focuses on the need to develop information systems as the first step in implementing information technology systems in the strategic and day-to-day running of any business. Discusses the subject of information itself, the different views of any information system and its key role in supporting the organization of any enterprise.

1992 *Computer-Integrated Construction Administration and Construction Management*, Cornick, T., Teaching Company Programme, Hans Haenlein Architects/University of Reading, Reading.
This is a recently-completed applied research project into the development of an integrated information support for design, construction management and the contract and business administration of a small architectural practice. The work demonstrated the fact that initially as much advantage is to be gained from integrating the information for the internal project management related to the practice business as integrating the building design and construction management processes through CAD-related systems. The ability to integrate the latter was also dependent on the characteristics of the CAD system being used.

1992 *IT Support System for Project Management*, Cornick, T., Teaching Company Programme, Scott Wilson Kirkpatrick/University of Reading, Reading.
This recently-completed applied research project looked at the development of a 'project management support system' for project managers within a large international engineering consultancy. The importance of ensuring that any computer-based system did actually support the management tasks of day-to-day running of projects was demonstrated. Standard database/spreadsheet application packages with minor modifications, supported by intensive IT staff training, proved to be the most successful approach.

1992 *Business Process Re-engineering Applied to Construction*, Koskela, L., Study at the Centre for Facilities Engineering, Stanford University, California.
A research study that proposes how the new philosophy of 'business process re-engineering' being applied in the manufacturing industries might be applied to the construction industry. It emphasizes the view that information flow is as important a part of any process as materials and that the re-engineered process should seek to minimize the variability and waste of both. IT is the enabling tool in this approach.

1993 *Implementing Simultaneous Engineering*, Conference supported by DTI, London.
This comprised three days of presentations and workshops demonstrating how the manufacturing industries were moving towards simultaneous or concurrent engineering in their efforts to reduce time and costly re-design in producing new products. This was being achieved, by and

large, by management reorganization into dynamic design and production teams – similar to the way that the construction industry has to build its products. The integration of product design and production was being achieved as much by management methods as by using IT tools and techniques.

1994   *The Successful Management of Design*, Gray, C., Hughes, W. and Bennett, J., The University of Reading, Reading.
A publicly-available report that describes the outcome of an industry-based study into the design management of modern building projects. Provides very practical guidance on managing the design of buildings where the design of the specialist trade contractor's 'engineered' element is vital to the building project design. Recognizes the uncertain and subjective nature of architectural design whilst stressing the importance of detail design control in order to produce correct and timely information for the management of building component production and construction assembly.

1994   *Computer-Aided Design for Construction in the Building Industry*, Luiten, G.T., Delft University of Technology, Delft.
A publicly-available report based on the work of six academic theses on the subject of Computer-Aided Design for Construction (CADfC). The research suggests a strategy for CADfC that takes account of three related points of view of an integration concept, computer implementation and organizational implementation. The results of the application of this strategy to practice through a case study suggest that integration of design and construction could be improved, to a limited extent, through knowledge and information exchange using object-orientated approaches.

1994   *First European Conference on Product and Process Modelling in the Building Industry*, the University of Technology, Dresden.
This comprises the conference papers on a European conference that brought together academic and industry-based researchers working in the area of product modelling for computer-based systems in the construction industry. It included applications in practice that ranged from management, design and construction control systems as well as robotics in construction. It also presented all the major EU-funded

projects on information integration in construction, some of which are described in outline in Appendix B.

1994 *Information Technology Support for Project and Business Management*, Cornick, T., Teaching Company Programme, Mouchel Ltd/University of Reading, Reading.

This is a current applied-research project (due for completion in October 1996) looking into ways of developing a company-wide integrated IT system to support the project and business management of a large international engineering consultancy. Many applications have been implemented using customized current and emerging applications. These all deal with, and will in the future integrate, such textual information systems that deal with client contacts, project quality plan and history, document management systems and others that will integrate and control the company's project and business processes. Outcomes so far suggest that using slightly modified standard applications will be beneficial.

1994 *CIB W88/96 Seminar – Architectural Management, Practice and Research*, Seminar Proceedings, Florence.

These are the proceedings of an international working group combining architectural management and quality assurance approaches for building. The papers suggest that architectural practice will have to become better managed in the future and as an activity, architectural design will have to become more integrated with the construction management processes involved in a building project. Scenarios concerning how IT will continue to make an impact upon conventional architectural practice are suggested and in particular how IT will change the way in which architects might conduct their business in the future.

1994 *The Art of the Structural Engineer*, Addis, B., Artemis, London.

A book based on examples of leading consulting engineer's designs for building forms. It successfully demonstrates and argues the case that structural engineers make an equally aesthetic contribution to a building's design as do architects. The form and fabric designed by the architect, and the services, all have to relate to the structural frame designed by the structural engineer. The need for engineers to become more involved in the actual production of their designs in the construction process is muted. The use of computers is seen as an essential tool in the analysis of even more aesthetically-interesting structural designs.

1994 *The Construction (Design and Management) Regulations 1994 (CDM).*
A new EU law introduced in order to improve construction health and safety, which requires that a building designer considers and assesses the health and safety risk involved the production of a proposed design. In doing this the designer will have to consult with a 'planning supervisor', whom the client has to legally appoint, and provide information for a 'safety plan' to be given to a 'principal contractor' in order to cost the construction.

1995 *The Autodesk University Event Conference*, London and the *AutoCad Applications Handbook*, CAD User Ltd, Kent.
An event organized by a leading CAD vendor that demonstrated the very practical possibilities of integration using currently and commercially-available CAD-related applications. Various cases were presented, using examples from both manufacturing and building industry applications, for directly integrating the CAD-generated manufacturing or building product form with various types of production and performance analysis tools. Building facility management and advanced visualization applications currently available to building clients, as well as architects, indicated possible changes in building procurement practice. New document management systems were also presented as providing support to design process control to meet quality assurance requirements and ensure legal code compliance.

The handbook demonstrates that a range of applications now exist in the marketplace that allow the integration of all critical factor analysis with the building design proposal either directly or indirectly, as it is generated using a CAD drawing system.

Index

Page numbers in **bold** refer to figures showing examples of computer drawings and other output. Page numbers in *italic* refer to items in the Bibliography.